Phlebotomy Test Prep: Exam Review Practice Questions

Volume Two

Jane John-Nwankwo   CPT, RN, MSN

PHLEBOTOMY TEST PREP: EXAM REVIEW PRACTICE QUESTIONS:
Volume Two

Copyright © 2013 by Jane John-Nwankwo RN, MSN

ISBN-13: 978-1490578996

ISBN-10: 1490578994

Printed in the United States of America.

In memory

In memory of my late father, John Chinyere Onwere who over-showered me with love in my childhood.

OTHER TITLES FROM THE SAME AUTHOR:

1. Director of Staff Development: The Nurse Educator

2. Crisis Prevention & Intervention in Healthcare: Management of Assaultive Behavior

3. CNA Exam Prep: Nurse Assistant Practice Test Questions. Vol. One and Two

4. Patient Care Technician Exam Review Questions: PCT Test Prep

5. IV Therapy & Blood Withdrawal Review Questions

6. Medical Assistant Test Preparation

7. EKG Test Prep

8. Phlebotomy Test Prep Vol One & Three

9. The Home Health Aide Textbook

10. How to make a million in nursing

   & More!

Order these books now at www.bestamericanhealthed.com/resources.html
Or call 951 637 8332 for bulk purchases

TABLE OF CONTENTS

SECTION ONE

1. One of the following has primary responsibility of protecting patients from hazards

   a. State Governor

   b. World Health Organization

   c. Health Workers

2. Invasion of the body by micro-organism like viruses, bacteria, fungi, etc. is known as

   a. Pain

   b. Infection

   c. Fatigue

3. One of the following microorganisms is normally found in the gastro-intestinal tract(GIT)

   a. Escherichia coli

   b. Herpes Virus

   c. Candida albicans

4. Blood-borne pathogens are infectious microorganisms present in _____?

   a. Air

   b. Water

c. Blood, tissue and body fluids

5. Microorganisms causing diseases are the following except

    a. Syphilis

    b. Ricin

    c. HIV (AIDS)

6. Aseptic techniques include the following except

    a. Handwashing

    b. Following standard precaution

    c. Bathing only when necessary

7. The following standards are upheld in the laboratory except one

    a. Eating, drinking and cosmetic application in the laboratory

    b. Assuming all specimens and patients are infectious

    c. Frequent hand hygiene

8. Food, drinks and bottled water can be kept in the refrigerator used for specimens

    and reagents. For they do not touch on another.

    a. True

    b. False

9. Safe work environment for health facilities and their workers are regulated by

    a. HIPA

b. OSHA

c. UNICEF

10. Disease that is transferred directly or indirectly from one person to another

through infectious organism is called

a. Hypertension

b. Communicable disease

c. Septicemia

11. Health-care Associated (Nosocomial) infections can be contracted in these hospitals

a. Postoperative Care Unit

b. Dialysis Unit

c. All of the above

12. When should incident of exposure to blood-borne pathogen be reported to the

supervisor?

a. Immediately

b. Not later than one week

c. Within one month

13. Surgical operation heightens susceptibility to infection because of this reason

a. Fear of surgery

b. Bacteria access to deeper tissue from wounds and drains

c. Restriction from eating food in the theatre

14. Following blood collection in isolation room, which of these personal protective equipment should be removed first

    a. Mask

    b. Gown

    c. Gloves

15. Clinical laboratory is vital in infection control in the following ways except

    a. Determining quality of sterilization and reporting on infectious agents

    b. Contamination of specimens occur in the laboratory

    c. Records in laboratory are used for surveillance

16. Bladder infection can result when Escherichia coli normally found in other parts of the body is transferred to bladder through poor hygiene

    a. True

    b. False

17. OSHA stipulates placing of warning labels on all containers for potentially infectious materials

    a. True

    b. False

18. Immediately after incident of exposure to blood-borne pathogens, employee is not expected to

    a. Clean with paper towel and forget about it

b. Decontaminate with soap and water or appropriate antiseptic

c. Flush the exposed mucus membrane into sterile saline water

19. Evaluation of exposed health care worker includes the following except

a. Confidential identification of the exposed health care worker and testing for the

HIV, hepatitis, with consent of the HCW)

b. Medical evaluation, counseling and post-exposure prophylaxis

c. Holding Conference to discuss careless attitude of the exposed worker

20. Nosocomial infection(health care related) occurs when chain of infection is

complete

a. True

b. False

21. Fomites like door knobs, water faucet handles, scrub suits, etc. found in healthcare

facilities are not important in transmission of pathogens

a. True

b. False

22. Reverse isolation or protective isolation is used to protect this group of patients

from infection

a. Immune compromised patients

b. Patients with Cellulitis

c. Young Patients

23. All containers for blood and potentially infectious materials must have warning

labels of which color

    a. Orange-red or fluorescent orange color

    b. Blue color

    c. White color

24. Accidental needle sticks can be prevented by following methods, except

    a. Activating safety device after using a needle

    b. Use of retractable puncture devices foe finger sticks

    c. Carefully attempting to re-cap needle

25. Which of the following is significant in a susceptible host of chain of infection

    a. Political affiliation

    b. Very young and very old (age)

    c. Skin color

26. The quicker the patient recovers, the better is the control of infection

    a. True

    b. False

27. Hand hygiene, immunization, good nutrition and proper exercise can be used to

interrupt nosocomial infection

    a. True

    b. False

28. Risk of transmission of microorganisms from known and unknown sources of infection in health facility in reduced by

    a. Engaging in sport activities

    b. Watching movies in hospital reception area

    c. Standard precaution

29. In addition to standard precautions, transmission based precautions are employed to control known or suspected infections

    a. True

    b. False

30. Hand washing technique stipulates vigorous rubbing of all surfaces of the hands for how long?

    a. At least 15 minutes

    b. At least 15 seconds

    c. At least 15 hours

31. If not using automatic or foot pedal control, a clean disposable towel can be used to turn off the faucet after hand washing

    a. True

    b. False

32. Infection control in the clinical laboratory can be achieved by which of the following

    a. Contact lenses should not be inserted or adjusted in the laboratory

b. Wearing of laboratory coat in lunchroom or at home should be avoided

c. All of the above

33. The following are factors affecting how susceptible a host is except

a. Financial Status

b. Underlying diseases like HIV (Aids), diabetes, etc.

c. Therapeutic interventions like chemotherapy, antibiotics, radiation, etc.

34. Breaking chain of infection at one or more links increases occurrence of infection

a. True

b. False

35. Spread of Tuberculosis is reduced by one of the following interventions

a. Love for intramuscular infections

b. Drinking clean water

c. Airborne precautions

36. Pneumonia, meningitis and rubella are diseases spread by

a. Airborne

b. Contact

c. Droplet

37. Which one of these is not a Personal Protective Equipment

a. Facial masks and gloves

b. Pen and marker

c. Respirators and gowns

38. A pair of gloves donned by a healthcare worker can be used on at least three patients before change

    a. True

    b. False

39. Glove removal should be immediately followed by washing of hand with soap and water or use of alcohol hand sanitizers

    a. True

    b. False

40. Select one that is not found in the chain of infection

    a. Susceptible host

    b. Immunization

    c. Source

41. Use of gloves is not necessary when examining infectious materials, wound drainages or fecal matter from known patients

    a. True

    b. False

42. Respiratory Syncytial virus (RSV), herpes simplex are spread through

    a. Contact

    b. Airborne

c. Droplet

43. The following are used during standard precautions except

   a. Glove

   b. Fan

   c. Hand hygiene

44. When hands are visibly soiled alcohol-based hand rub is only recommended for

   decontamination of hands

   a. True

   b. False

45. Droplet precautions are used for droplets smaller than 5 microns

   a. True

   b. False

46. When droplets are smaller than 5 microns airborne precautions are used

   a. True

   b. False

47. Frequent glove change after 30 minutes is necessary because gloves can become

   permeable or dissolve with sweaty hands or other chemicals in clinical laboratory

   environment

   a. True

   b. False

48. Newborns are susceptible to infections because their immune systems are not yet fully developed

    a. True

    b. False

49. Babies whose mother has which of these must be isolated from others

    a. Headache

    b. Hypertension

    c. Genital Herpes

50. The acronym CDC stands for

    a. Completing difficult computer test

    b. Center for disease control and prevention

    c. Common duties for commuters and drivers

51. Personal Protection Equipment (PPE) include the following except

    a. Gown

    b. Respirator

    c. Stethoscope

SECTION TWO

1. Hazards in healthcare facilities are the following

    a. Radioactive effects and mechanical hazards from equipment

b. Hazards from specimens, reagents and allergies to latex material

c. All of the above

2. In order to ensure fire safety, employees of health facilities should be conversant in the following

a. Location and use of fire extinguishers and fire blankets

b. Sound knowledge of procedure to follow during fire outbreak

c. All of the above

3. Fire has 3 general classifications namely

a. Class X, Class Y and Class Z

b. Class A, Class B and Class C

c. Class P, Class Q and Class R

4. The acronym RACE stands for

a. Rescue, Alert, Confine and Extinguish

b. Rest, Assist, Confront and Evacuate

c. Rebuke, Adjust, Condemn and Explain

5. It is a daily responsibility to protect clients, health workers and visitors from hazards

a. True

b. False

6. If fire or explosion arise in health facility don't do which of the following

a. Block the exit and entrances

b. Run, panic and jump up and down

c. All of the above

7. In an organized version, healthcare workers should follow this acronym (as guide if there is a fire outbreak)

a. RACE

b. RICE

c. ABC

8. When putting out fire, extinguishers should be aimed at what part of the fire

a. Base of the fire

b. Top of the fire

c. Middle and flame of the fire

9. If caught in fire, crawling out is advised because

a. It is good to imitate kids

b. Breathing is better at the floor as smoke rises high

c. Crawling does not make fire look so serious

10. It is safe to use electrical appliances that are soaked with water and liquid

a. True

b. False

11. During blood withdrawal s contact with electrical appliance can shock patients when electricity passes through you and needle to patient

    a. True

    b. False

12. In order to ensure proper equipment grounding. Identify appropriate "hospital grade" electrical plugs to be used

    a. One-prong electrical plug

    b. Two-prong electrical plug

    c. Three-prong electrical plug

13. In case of electrical accident , victim should not be rescued with bare hand

    a. True

    b. False

14. It is extremely important to do which of the following immediately there is an electrical accident

    a. Shut off electrical power source

    b. Increase the power voltage

    c. Look for cell phone to call 911

15. The following methods are used to rescue in case of fire accident

    a. Remove electrical contact from victim with materials that do not conduct electricity eg glass breaker

b. Shut off electrical power source

c. All of the above

16. Healthcare workers should anticipate to start which procedure after rescuing

victim of electrical shock

   a. Administer prescribed injections

   b. Cardiopulmonary resuscitation

   c. Check blood pressure and visual acuity

17. Identify the three cardinal principles of self- protection from exposure to

radiation

   a. Organic food, appropriate weight, fluid intake

   b. Distance, shielding and time

   c. Good diet, exercise, immunization

18. It is always good to conceal warning signs for radioactive materials

   a. True

   b. False

19. Which of the following is appropriate for a place where radioactive materials are

used or kept

   a. Traffic signs posted on the entrance of the door

   b. Love signs posted on the entrance of the door

   c. Warning signs posted on the entrance of the door

20. It is a waste of time to properly label radioactive reagents and specimens

    a. True

    b. False

21. Healthcare workers muse wear which of the following when he works in section with high radioactivity to determine amount received

    a. Dosimeter badge

    b. Professional badge

    c. Police badge

Potential hazards

22. Radiation exposure hazards can be encountered by healthcare worker in the following ways, except

    a. Collecting specimens from patients in x-ray or nuclear medicine department

    b. Taking specimens to radioimmunoassay unit

    c. Working in emergency unit of the health facility

23. The following diseases are caused by high exposure to radioactivity, except

    a. Malang

    b. Leukemia

    c. Cancer of various types

24. This group of health workers are prevented from working in units with potential radiation hazards

    a. Post- menopausal women

    b. Pregnant women

    c. Women between 20 to 30 years of age

25. Dosimeter badge should be read periodically as per facility's policy

    a. True

    b. False

26. Incorrect use and maintenance of centrifuge instrument is not important provided patient is not aware of it

    a. True

    b. False

27. Label on reagent should be carefully read before using it because of these reasons, except

    a. To know content of the container

    b. Only for examination purpose

    c. To know degree of hazards that can ensue from the reagent or chemical

28. One of these may be one of the most important activities in chemical handling

    a. Keeping chemicals in black containers

    b. Placing chemicals transparent containers

c. Proper labeling of chemicals

29. Which of these is not ponds of qualities of an acceptable chemical labels

    a. It must be written in foreign language

    b. It must have a clear waning and special precautions

    c. It must provide first-aid intervention in case of exposure to the chemical

30. Water should never be added to acid

    a. True

    b. False

31. Acid should never be added to water

    a. True

    b. False

32. Personal protective equipment like buttoned laboratory coat necessary when handling chemicals

    a. True

    b. False

33. These are useful protective measures for use or chemical except

    a. Do not store chemical above eye level

    b. Use of personal protective equipment

    c. Do not read labels on chemicals

34. Warning signs is required in any room where chemical is stored

 a. True

 b. False

35. When transporting strong acids, alkalis, and hazardous substance, the following method should not be used

 a. Use of bare hand

 b. Use of container specially designed for the purpose

 c. Proper labeling of the container

36. No chemical should be stored in containers that is unlabeled

 a. True

 b. False

37. Accidental chemical spill on body parts should be followed immediately with

 a. At least 15 seconds of rinsing with water

 b. At least 5 minutes of rinsing with water

 c. At least 15 minutes of rinsing with water

38. During immediate response after accidental chemical spill in the eye, vigorous rubbing of eye is not advised because of which of the following

 a. It will only result in temporary relief

 b. It will cause further damage to the eye

 c. It will destroy contact lenses

39. To ensure through eye cleansing which of these items must be removed before starting rinsing

    a. Contact lenses

    b. Remote control

    c. A pair of shoes

40. Which of the following item is not needed in case of chemical spill cleanup

    a. Spill cleanup kit containing absorbents and neutralizers

    b. Personal protective equipment like rubber gloves, ect.

    c. Anatomy and physiology textbook

41. Healthcare worker is aware of these in the place of work, except

    a. Procedures accepted for cleaning up chemical spill

    b. Age of newly employed staff in the unit

    c. Emergency phone number to contact at the facility

42. Identify what healthcare worker may not report to nursing station immediately

    a. Blood back up in line to the container

    b. When infusion alarm goes off and swelling at insertion site

    c. When patient smiles to healthcare worker

43. The following can be responsible for shipping hazards to patients and healthcare workers, except

    a. Sounds from televisions

b. Leaks from intravenous line

c. Urine spill and food particles

44. Expression of pain, sudden unconsciousness does not warrant informing nurses

immediately because patients may be pretending

    a. True

    (b.) False

45. Running in health facility may not be responsible for which of the following

    (a.) Terrorist attack in foreign country

    b. Patients and visitors may be alarmed and start to run

    c. Healthcare worker carrying specimen tray may be hurt with patient

    walking in the hallway

46. Flowers, petals, ladders, trays and cart flittered around hallway can result

potential hazards to patients and healthcare workers

    (a.) True

    b. False

47. Signs and symptoms of allergic reaction to latex are the following, except

    a. Shock and sinus irritability

    b. Skin rash, hives and eye irritation

    (c.) Hypertension and Malang

48. This, among the items listed below may not contain latex

a. Rubber apron, iv tubing and injection port

b. Tourniquets, rubber gloves, and urinary catheter

c. Blankets, wooden chairs and health facility brochure

49. Healthcare worker has just received a bomb threat call, he is not expected to do which of these

   a. Keep it secret so as not to terrify patients and co-workers

   b. Allow caller to speak noting his language, location and background noise

   c. Document what caller says about bomb location, denotation time and inform security department

50. In case of emergency everybody should work to achieve the following except

   a. Send for medical assistance

   b. Be the first person to address the press and take picture

   c. Prevent bleeding, ensure clear airway, prevent shock and further injury

51. Bleeding is prevented in emergency situations with the following methods, except

   a. Putting clean cloth on wound and insert pressure with gloved hand

   b. Extremities not fractured can be lifted above victims heart

   c. Pouring sand or food particles on the wound

52. In order to stop bleeding tourniquet can be used on amputated severity

    mangled and crushed leg

    a. True

    b. False

53. Every healthcare worker should be able to demonstrate basic CPR techniques

    a. First time at emergency scene

    b. Only after learning from emergency situation

    c. Before emergency situation

54. Shock may be prevented in emergency situation by doing the following, expect

    a. Prevention of bleeding and hypothermia

    b. Prevention of thirst by giving oral fluids to patients at emergency scene

    c. Prevention of insufficient oxygen supply to victim

55. Tapping the victim gently to determine if they are conscious occupies which step

    in giving breathing aid

    a. First step in breathing aid

    b. Second step in breathing aid

    c. Third step in breathing aid

56. Which of this is the most common difficulty with ventilation breathing aid

    a. Rescuer may be too tall

    b. Short height of the rescuer

c. Poor chin and head positioning

SECTION THREE

1. Control center of cell structure is known as

   a. Mitochondria

   b. Cytoplasm

   c. Nucleus

2. _____ is the incision or cut into the vein

   a. Laparotomy

   b. Phlebotomy

   c. Osteotomy

3. Inflammation of the inside lining of the heart is known as

   a. Endocarditis

   b. Osteitis

   c. Cellulitis

4. The meaning of prefix hyper is _____

   a. Below or under

   b. Above and excessive

   c. Beside

5. Examples of germ cells are the following, except

   a. Neurons

b. Ova

c. Spermatozoa

6. Condition in which bone becomes porous is _____

   a. Osteomyelitis

   b. Estrogen

   c. Osteoporosis

7. Prefix brady implies _____

   a. Destroy

   b. Double

   c. Delay

8. Prefix dipl means what

   a. Destroy

   b. Double

   c. Delay

9. What is percentage of water in human body weight

   a. Ninety percent

   b. Thirty percent

   c. Forty percent

10. _____ is the suffix that means surgical excision

    a. Embrace

b. Embalm

c. Ectomy

11. The study of structure and functions of cell is called

    a. Chemistry

    b. Cytology

    c. Physics

12. The following are parts of functions of the skeletal systems, except

    a. Hemopoesis (blood cell formation)

    b. Support, calcium store

    c. Earing and taste

13. Intake of oxygen (O2) and expiration of carbon dioxide CO2 in the body is

    function of which of the following systems?

    a. Reproductive system

    b. Respiratory system

    c. Digestive system

14. Organs found in respiratory system are these

    a. Iris, retina, vitreous humour

    b. Epidermis, dermis, subcutaneous

    c. Pharynx, trachea, bronchi, and alyeoti

15. Erythrocyte means_____

a. Red blood cells

b. Random blood sugar

c. Erectile tissue

16. The suffix –emesis is known as

a. Emblem

b. Vomiting

c. Mansion

17. Study of blood and blood- forming tissue is known as _____

a. Hematology

b. Hydrology

c. Agricultural science

18. _____ is the study of microbes

a. Theology

b. Enthomolog

c. Microbiology

19. Skin is colored by what substance in the body

a. Blood

b. Hormone

c. Melanin

20. Ophthalmology is the study that pertains to diseases of which part of the body

a. Open wound

b. Eye

c. Live

21. The study of physical structure of human body is called

    a. Physiology

    b. Anatomy

    c. Anthropology

22. The study of functional process of human body is known as

    a. Physiology

    b. Physics

    c. Fine art

23. Study of disease- causing agents is called

    a. Nephrology

    b. Psychiatry

    c. Pathology

24. What is homeostasis

    a. Static homes

    b. Poor flow of blood

    c. Steady- state condition

25. Genetic blueprint is controlled by

a. Spermatozoa

(b.) Deoxyribonucleic Acid (DNA)

c. Growth hormone

26._____ is the principal source of cellular energy

(a.) Mitochondria

b. Endoplasmic reticulum

c. Lysosomes

27._____ is an important aspect of homeostasis when healthy body makes

necessary substances

a. Digestion

b. Movement

(c.) Metabolism

28.The outer covering of cell is _____

a. Cilia

(b.) Cell membrane

c. Cytoplasm

29.Homeostasis or normal functioning of the body can be assessed by health care

worker by taking

(a.) Vital signs

b. Patients previous phone calls

c. Dressing pattern of the patient

30. Identify the organs that are found in abdominopelyic cavity

    a. Thumbs and hairs

    b. Stomach and small intestines

    c. Breast and sternum

31. Spinal cord is encased in which of these cavities

    a. Cranial cavity

    b. Abdominal cavity

    c. Spinal cavity

32. "Vital signs" is basically comprise of the following, except

    a. Hormone assay

    b. Pulse and respiration rate

    c. Temperature and blood pressure

33. The term used to described the front part of the human body is _____

    a. Inferior

    b. Posterior

    c. Anterior

34. Part of the body towards the back is described with the term

    a. Anterior

    b. Posterior

c. Medical

35. Normal anatomic positions is described as with of the following where body-

    a. Stands erct with arms at rest and palms facing forwards

    b. Stops down, with arms elevated and palms facing forwards

    c. Sits on the chair with arms at rest

36. Venipuncture can be performed on patient who is standing

    a. True

    b. False

37. Risk of fainting and falling is higher in patient when venipuncture is which

    position

    a. Supine position

    b. Sitting position

    c. Normal anatomic position

38. The best position encouraged to perform phlebotomy on patients who are in

    bed is _____

    a. Supine position- lying on his back with face up

    b. Prone position- lying his stomach with face down

    c. Lateral position- lying on his side(left or right)

39. Proximal is term used to described the point

    a. Above the point of attachment

b. Besides the point of attachment

(c.) Near the point of attachment

40. "Deep" is used to described a point far from the surface of the body

(a) True

b. False

41. When a vein is described as superficial, it shows that the vein is

a. Hidden from the naked eye

b. Far from the surface of the body

(c.) Near the surface of the body

42. Cranial cavity contains what

a. Spinal cord

(b) Brain

c. Bone marrow

43. The following organs are found in thoracic cavity

(a) Lungs and the heart

b. Liver and kidney

c. Kidney and bladder

44. Prone position (lying face down) is not recommended for phlebotomy because

a. Patient will not see the procedure

(b) Orientation of the arms are awkward

c. Blood does not flow when patient is lying face down

45. The root word "angio" is referring to what?

a. Vessel

b. Bone

c. Skin

46. Healthcare worker must always refer to patients sides in vein assessment, not health care workers guide

a. True

b. False

47. Can you identify one reason why healthcare workers must not confuse patient's left and right side with his own left and right?

a. Skin color may be different between left and right hand side

b. Clinical conditions on a side of the body may determine specific instructions on procedure

c. One side may have longer extremities than the other

48. The directional term "proximal" means

a. No relationship with the point of reference

b. Far from the point of reference

c. Clear to the point of reference

49. Directional term used for away from the point of reference is called

a. Peripheral

b. Proximal

c. Distal

50. Superficial refers to_____

   a. At surface of the body

   b. Inside the body

   c. Inside the bone

51. The cheek region of the body is called

   a. Buccal region

   b. Brachial region

   c. Cubital region

52. Cervical region is also known as_____

   a. Abdominal region

   b. Leg region

   c. Meek region

53. Digital region of the body is synonymous with

   a. Fingers

   b. Bones

   c. Eyes

54. Upper arm is a location known as

a. Buccal region

b. Brachial region

c. Breast

55. The word "plantar" is referring to

a. Armpit

b. Sole of foot

c. Knee

56. Nasal region is referring to what

a. Nose

b. Knee

c. Skin

57. Forearm is the same as_____region

a. Sternal region

b. Axillary region

c. Ante brachial region

58. Eye area is a location also known as

a. Gluteal region

b. Orbital region

c. Nasal region

59. Pedal region is located in which part of the body

a. Eye

b. Anus

c. Foot

60. Femoral region is the same as

a. Upper inner thigh

b. Face

c. Neck

61. Buttocks is called

a. Mouth

b. Gluteal region

c. Breast bone

62. Mouth is synonymous with

a. Digital region

b. Nasal region

c. Oral region

63. Breast bone area is also called

a. Femoral region

b. Sternal region

c. Buccal region

64. Which of the terminology is appropriate location for the chest

a. Thoracic

b. Pubic

c. Lumbar

65. Specific measurable state with chemical symptoms patient history and laboratory or other investigation result is called

a. Disease

b. Politics

c. Prayer

66. The term illness is a subjective, unspecific decision from wellness

a. True

b. False

67. The following are specific functions of clinical laboratory test, except

a. Screening of disease like diabetes, etc.

b. Diagnosis of infections eg. Sexually transmitted diseases

c. Advertisement of health facility

68. Clinical laboratory test like drug levels in the serum does not help in the treatment of patients

a. True

b. False

69. Monitoring of progress achieved in the treatment of disease in possible with chemical laboratory test

   a. True

   b. False

70. Support, movement and formation of the body framework is a major function of which of this organ systems

   a. Digestive systems

   b. Cardiovascular systems

   c. Skeletal system

71. The following are the functions of the nervous systems, except

   a. Storage of urine

   b. Transmission of impulses and response to change

   c. Communication and control over all body parts

72. Elimination of stool is a basic function of

   a. Skeletal system

   b. Urinary system

   c. Digestive system

73. Inspiration of oxygen (O2) and elimination of gaseous waste like carbon dioxide(CO2) is a function of

   a. Respiratory system

b. Integumentary system

c. Reproductive system

74. Integumentary system(skin) has the following functions, except

a. Temperature regulation and sensory function

b. Produces urine and regulates blood clotting

c. Protection from harsh condition and invasion of microbes

75. Veins and arteries are integrated parts of

a. Endocrine system

b. Cardiovascular system

c. Nervous system

76. This organ is responsible for heat projection, posture and movement

a. Muscular system

b. Lymphatic system

c. Cardiovascular system

77. What is the name of the substance that provides color of skin and prevent

absorption of ultraviolet rays

a. Menstrual flow

b. Marijuana

c. Melanin

78. Hair provides which of the following functions

a. Heat insulator

b. Digestion of food

c. Age determination

79. Eyelashes does not protect eye from foreign bodies in any way

a. True

b. False

80. Skin layers are in this order from superficial to deep

a. Epidermis, subcutaneous, dermis

b. Subcutaneous, epidermis, dermis

c. Epidermis, dermis, subcutaneous

81. Number of bones in the body is believed to be around

a. 16

b. 206

c. 76

82. Bone does not have blood supply at all

a. True

b. False

83. Most blood cells are produced in

a. Bone joints

b. Bone periosteum

c. Bone marrow

84. Beak in continuity of bone is known as

   a. Bone fracture

   b. Bone fertility

   c. Bone loss

85. The following are common laboratory test for skeletal systems, except

   a. Stool blood occult

   b. Serum phosphate level

   c. Vitamin D level

86. _____ is the longest bone in the body

   a. Frontal bone

   b. Femur

   c. Clavicle

87. One of these is not a classification of muscles

   a. Cardiac muscle

   b. Skeletal muscle

   c. Kidney muscle

88. Voluntary muscles are attached to

   a. Nails

   b. Heart

c. Bones

89. Muscles of the heart are called

a. Cardial muscles

b. Cardiovascular muscles

c. Voluntary muscles

90. One of these is not among laboratory tests for the muscular system

a. Biopsy tissue microscopic test

b. Autoimmune antibodies analysis

c. Complete blood cells count (CBC)

91. Nervous system consists of the following, except

a. Brain

b. Kidney

c. Spinal cord

92. _____ is the fluid found in the spinal cavity

a. Cerebrospinal fluid

b. Aqueous humours

c. Tear

93. Brain and spinal cord are covered by

a. Meninges

b. Melanin

c. Skin

94. Nerves that control muscles of hand, arm, and shoulder are located

   a. Cervical 5 through thoracic 1

   b. Lumber 5 through sacrum

   c. Lumbers through coccyx

95. In superior- inferior fashion, vertebral bones are arranged in this order

   a. Cervical, thoracic, coccyx, lumber, sacrum

   b. Cervical, thoracic, sacrum, lumber, coccyx

   c. Cervical, thoracic, lumber, sacrum, coccyx

96. Nervous system includes of one of these

   a. Neurons

   b. Nails

   c. Knee

97. Pick one that is not related to nervous system

   a. Encephalitis and meningitis

   b. Epilepsy and hydrocephaly

   c. Tendinitis and urethritis

98. Respiratory system can be found in the lower and upper extremities

   a. True

   b. False

99. Respiratory system organs are found in which of the following

   a. Hair, nails, and bones

   b. Legs, arms, and liver

   c. Head, neck, chest

100. Human beings has how may lungs

   a. 4 lungs

   b. 2 lungs

   c. 3 lungs

101. One of the following statement is true about the lungs

   a. Right lung has 3 lobes and the left lung has 2 lobes

   b. Right lung has 2 lobes and the left has 3 lobes

   c. Right and left lung have 3 lobes

102. Which of these groups is not forms in respiratory organ system

   a. Nose, pharynx, and bronchi

   b. Larynx, bronchi, and lungs

   c. Kidney, liver, and spleen

103. Identify one incorrect order among respiratory organ system

   a. Nose- lungs- larynx

   b. Trachea- bronchi- lungs

   c. Nose- pharynx- larynx

104. In the exchange of gases, which of the following is correct

   a. A person breaths in O2 and breaths out CO2

   b. A person breaths in CO2 and breaths out O2

   c. A person breaths in CO2 and never needs O2

105. Exchange of gases occurs in

   a. Trachea

   b. Larynx

   c. Alveoli

106. Normal body PH ranges within _____

   a. 7.15 and 7.25

   b. 7.25 and 7.35

   c. 7.35 and 7.45

107. Identify and pick the correct statement

   a. As CO2 levels increases, blood PH increases

   b. As CO2 level increases, blood PH decreases

   c. As CO2 level increases, blood PH remains stagnant

108. Infections conditions of the respiratory organ system are these, except

   a. Asthma

   b. Tuberculosis

   c. Pneumonia

109. Episode an highly reversible cough, difficulty in breathing and chest tightness

is called

a. Tuberculosis

b. Asthma

c. Pneumonia

110. Pneumonia is defined as

a. Inflammation of the abdomen

b. Inflammation of the neck

c. Inflammation of the lung tissue

111. The inflammation of the bronchus is called

a. Bronchitosis

b. Bronchitis

c. Busitus

112. The following are laboratory tes on respiratory systems except

a. Blood PH and gases (CO_2 and O_2)

b. Urine Culture

c. Sputum Culture

113. One of the highlighted test helps in the assessment of lung tissue

a. Lung Biopsies

b. Throat swabs

c. Sputum Culture

114. Hepatitis is the inflammation of the

a. Kidney

b. Head

c. Liver

115. Mouth and teeth are not parts of the digestive system

a. True

b. False

116. Involuntary movement of food through the gastrointestinal tract is called

a. Peristalsis

b. Swallowing

c. Mastication

117. Digestion of _____ starts in the mouth with the help of saliva

a. Fat and Oil

b. Protein

c. Carbohydrates

118. Which of these conditions is irreversible

a. Asthma

b. Emphysema

c. Pneumonia

119. The pathogenic organism causing ulcer and cancers of stomach and intestines is called

a. Helicopter pylori

b. Helicobacter pylori

c. Chooper pylori

120. Identify one that is not found in the digestive systems

a. Diverticulitis

b. Appendicitis

c. Tinea Capitis

121. The group that is found a parasite in the digestive system is

a. Hookworm, tapeworm, and roundworm (ascaris)

b. Cholera, Typhoid fever, Appendicitis

c. Colitis, constipation and hemorrhoid

122. Colitis is inflammation of

a. Larynx

b. Colon

c. Gum

123. The following tests are peculiar to digestive system except

a. Bacteria culture

b. Glucose tolerance test

c. Urine Culture

124. Stool analysis for ova and parasites has nothing to do with the digestive system

a. True

b. False

125. Analysis of stomach content to determine quality of secretion, free and combined

hydrochloric acid, blood, bile acid etc. is called

a. Gastric Analysis

b. Garlic Analysis

c. Barium Meal

126. The terminal component of urinary system is called

a. Urinometer

b. Ureter

c. Urethra

127. The under listed organs are in pairs (two) except

a. Bladder

b. Urethra

c. Kidney

128. Identify correct order of urinary organ systems

a. Kidney-ureter-urethra-bladder

b. kidney-bladder-ureter-urethra

c. kidney-ureters-bladder-urethra

129. Inflammation of the urinary bladder is called

a. Bursitus

b. Cystitis

c. Blastocyst

130. The normal ratio of carbonic acid to bicarbonate (base) is

a. 1:10

b. 1:20

c. 1:30

131. Acidosis is the condition in which blood PH is less than

a. 7.35

b. 7.25

c. 7.45

132. Alkalosis is the condition in which blood PH is

a. less than 7.25

b. less than 7.35

c. greater than 7.45

133. Enlarged thyroid gland is called

a. Gangrene

b. Goiter

c. Gastrin

134. The pituitary gland is often called

a. Master Gland

b. Mother Gland

c. Sister Gland

135. Exocrine gland secretes its contents through

a. Directly into the blood stream

b. Into the air

c. Through channel

136. Endocrine gland secretes its hormones

a. Through the stomach into the duodenum

b. Directly into the bloodstream

c. Directly into the brain

137. Which one of these is not among disorders of the endocrine system

a. Addison's Disease

b. Graves' Disease

c. Gravel's Disease

138. Erthropoetin is produced in the

a. Blood

(b) Kidney

c. Bone Marrow

139. Male and Female reproductive systems are not the same

(a). True

b. False

140. The following are sexually transmitted disease

a. Hypertension and Migrane

b. Cellulitis and gangrene

(c) Gonorrhea and syphilis

SECTION FOUR

1. Identify the one that is not component of cardiovascular system

   (a) Eustachian Tube

   b. Heart and blood vessels

   c. Circulatory blood

2. The heart is about the size of

   a. Adult's head

   (b) Adult's fist

c. Adult's kidney

3. Heart is a hollow_____ organ

   a. cartilaginous

   b. bony

   c. muscular

4. The vessel that transports blood form the heart to entire body is called

   a. Venules

   b. artery

   c. vein

5. _____ transport blood from part of the body back to the heart

   a. Arterioles

   b. arteries

   c. veins

6. _____ are the microscopic vessels that connect arterioles and

venules together

   a. Gastrointestinal tract

   b. Capillaries

   c. Nostril

7. Veins transport _____ blood to the lungs

   a. Deoxygenated

b. Oxygenated

8. Walls of veins are _____

    a. Have a pulse

    b. Thicker than arteries and appear red

    c. thinner than arteries and appear bluish

9. Which one of these is not a characteristic of an artery

    a. contains valves for preventing back flow of blood

    b. it has pulse

    c. it has thicker and highly elastic walls than vein

10. Functions of circulatory blood are the following except

    a. Production of hormones for physiological activities

    b. Transportation of oxygen and Carbon dioxide

    c. Movement and distribution of fluids and nutrients

11. The location of the heart is called

    a. Periosteum

    b. Mediasternum

    c. Ileum

12. How many chambers does the heart have?

    a. 2

    b. 3

c. ④

13. Right atrium receives

    a. oxygen-rich blood

    b. oxygen-poor blood

    c. none of the above

14. _____convey deoxygenated blood from right ventricle to the

lungs for oxygenation

    a. Aorta

    b. left and right pulmonary arteries

    c. left and right pulmonary veins

15. Mediastinum is found in which cavity of the body?

    a. pelvic cavity

    b. abdominal cavity

    c. thoracic cavity

16. Newly oxygenated blood is transported from the lungs to left atrium

by

    a. left and right pulmonary veins

    b. left and right pulmonary arteries

    c. left and right renal arteries

17. Oxygenated blood leaves left ventricle through _____ to all parts of the body

   a. the aorta

   b. the left and right pulmonary arteries

   c. superior vena cava

18. _____ is the valve between right atrium and right ventricle

   a. Quadcuspid valve

   b. tricuspid valve

   c. bicuspid valve

19. Inbetween the left atrium and left ventricle is

   a. mitral valve

   b. mediteranean valve

   c. medium valve

20. Given the high contraction needed to pump blood to all parts of the body

   a. left and right ventricle are the same thickness

   b. left ventricle is thinner that right ventricle

   c. left ventricle is thicker than right ventricle

21. The contraction of the heart is called _____

   a. diastole

b. systole

c. pulse

22. Relaxation of the heart is called _____

    a. systole

    b. diastole

    c. pulse

23. Average heart beats in a healthy and resting adult is

    a. 55-60 beats per minute

    b. 100-120 beats per minute

    c. 60-80 beats per minute

24. Identify a group of blood vessels

    a. Eustachian tube, larynx, trachea

    b. capillaries, veins, arteries

    c. osteoblast, osteoclast,

25. _____ are the largest veins in human body

    a. right and left femoral veins

    b. superior and inferior vena cava

    c. anterior and posterior tibial veins

26. _____ vessels carry blood away from the heart

    a. afferent vessels

b. efferent vessels

c. mixed vessels

27. Pulmonary veins carry

    a. Deoxygenated blood

    b. Arterial blood

    c. oxygenated blood

28. Vessels carrying blood towards the heart are called _____

    a. afferent vessels

    b. cardiac vessels

    c. efferent vessels

29. All arteries carry oxygenated blood except

    a. pulmonary arteries

    b. femoral arteries

    c. renal arteries

30. Loss of elasticity and contractibility of an artery is called

    a. atherosclerosis

    b. artifact

    c. arteriosclerosis

31. Accumulation of plaque that reduces the lumen diameter is called

    a. artifact

b. atherosclerosis

c. arterosclerosis

32. _____ is the most commonly used are for venipuncture

    a. antecubital are of forearm

    b. scalp area

    c. Plantar venous network

33. A typical structure of artery or vein has how many layers

    a. 1

    b. 2

    c. 3

34. Atheromatous plaque predisposes a patient to blood clot formation

    a. true

    b. false

35. _____ is the best vein for venipuncture at the ante cubital area

    a. cephalic vein

    b. median cubital vein

    c. basilic vein

36. _____ vein is found in almost full length of the arm

    a. median cubital vein

    b. cephalic vein

c. brachial vein

37. _____ is the link vein between basilic and cephalic vein

    a. brachial vein

    b. ulnar vein

    c. median cubital vein (superficial)

38. _____ is the longest vein in the human body

    a. common iliac vein

    b. brachial vein

    c. greater saphenous vein

39. Veinous blood is dark red in color because _____

    a. it is rich in oxygen

    b. it is poor in oxygen

    c. it has less blood cells

40. Backflow of blood is prevented in veinous blood because

    a. veinous blood does not travel against gravity

    b. vein contains valve that prevents blood replux

    c. volume of veinous blood is always less

41. It is easier to stop arterial bleeding than veinous bleeding

    a. true

    b. false

42. Arterial bleeding reveals blood that is bright red because the blood is rich in oxygen

   a. true

   b. false

43. _____ is the condition in which a tissue is deficient in blood and oxygen supply

   a. hypoxia

   b. hypertension

   c. hypotension

44. Whole blood contains _____

   a. 25% plasma and 75% of cells

   b. 45% plasma and 55% of cells

   c. 55% plasma and 45% of cells

45. Average adult man has about _____ liters of blood

   a. 5 liters

   b. 50 liters

   c. 500 liters

46. Plasma portion of blood contains

   a. 50% of solutes and 50% of water

   b. 8% of solutes and 92% of water

c. 80% of solutes and 20% of water

47. White blood cells are subdivided into _____

   a. granulocyes and agranulocytes

   b. pure shite and impure white

   c. regular and irregular

48. Cellular components of blood are divided to how many

   a. 3

   b. 1

   c. 2

49. About 99% of blood cells are

   a. leukocytes

   b. erythrocytes

   c. platelets

50. The cellular content of blood that is responsible for clotting is _____

   a. erythrocytes

   b. platelets

   c. leukocytes

51. Oxygen carrying capacity of blood is present in _____

   a. platelets

   b. leukocytes

c. erythrocytes

52. Blood helps in redistribution of heat throughout the body

    a. true

    b. false

53. _____ is defined as non-nucleated bioconcaved disks

    a. leukocytes

    b. erythrocytes

    c. platelets

54. _____ is the process for formation of red blood cells

    a. erythropoiesis

    b. photosynthesis

    c. hydrolysis

55. Average life span of a red blood cell is

    a. 200 days

    b. 12 days

    c. 120 days

56. The diameter of an erythrocyte is about

    a. 7cm

    b. 7mm

    c. 7um

57. _____ is the name of hormone formed in the kidney that stimulate production of erythrocytes

   a. erythropoietin

   b. growth hormone

   c. adrenalin

58. _____ is the iron-containing pigments found after hemoglobin breakdown

   a. hemopoetin

   b. hemolysis

   c. hemosiderin

59. Blood types found in humans are

   a. X,Y,W,Z

   b. A,B,AB,O

   c. P,Q,R,S

60. The most common blood type is

   a. Type O

   b. Type Z

   c. Type R

61. Presence or absence of antigens and antibodies in blood determines blood type

a. True

b. False

62. Type A blood will have A antigens on the surface of its erythrocytes (rbc) and anti-B antibodies in its plasma

    a. True

    b. False

63. Type O blood is called

    a. Union Blood

    b. United Emirate

    c. Universal Donor

64. _____ can be administered during and after first pregnancy to prevent Hemolytic Disease of the newborn

    a. RhoGam

    b. Rhode

    c. Tylenol

65. Blood reactions mostly occur in the first

    a. 15 hours

    b. 15 minutes

    c. 15 days

66. _____ fights against pathogenic organisms in the body

a. Leukocytes

b. Erythrocytes

c. Platelets

67. Blood usually contains

a. 1,000-3,000 leukocytes/mm3

b. 5,000-10,000 leukocytes/mm3

c. 12,000-15,000 leukocytes/mm3

68. The smallest blood cells are

a. Platelets

b. Leukocytes

c. Erythrocytes

69. _____ is the life span of a platelet

a. 90-100 days

b. 1-8 days

c. 9-12 days

70. There are about _____ platelets in circulating blood

a. 5,000-25,000/mm3

b. 250,000-500,000/mm3

c. 25,0000-50,000/mm3

71. Low platelets counts is called

a. Oliguria

b. Thrombocytopenia

c. Alopecia

72. Thrombocytosis is

a. Excessive platelets counts

b. Low platelet counts

c. Medium platelets counts

73. The following medications can predispose patients to excessive

bleeding except

a. cumadin

b. heparin

c. Vitamin B Complex

74. Complete blood count (CBC) refers to all blood cell counts

a. True

b. False

75. Normal Hemoglobin (Hgb) range in female is

a. 20-30 g/100ml

b. 12-16 g/100ml

c. 70-90 g/100ml

76. Hematocrit in male ranges between _____

a. 5%-10%

b. 10%-20%

c. 40%-54%

77. Red Blood Cells count(RBC) in female is

a. 1-3 million/mm3

b. 4-5 million/mm3

c. 7-8 million/mm3

78. Creatinine level in blood is normally

a. 3-4 mg/dl

b. 0.6-1.2 mg/dl

c. 9-10 mg/dl

79. Normal fasting blood sugar is

a. 70-110 mg/dl

b. 120-200 mg/dl

c. 40-50 mg/dl

80. Calcium (Ca) level in blood is

a. 9.2-11.0 mg/dl

b. 7.0-8.0 mg/dl

c. 6.0-7.0 mg/dl

81. Two-hour postprandial glucose is

a. 140 mg/dl

b. 70 mg/dl

c. 50 mg/dl

82. Sodium (NA) level in blood is

    a. 136-142 mmol/L

    b. 2-3 mmol/L

    c. 25-40 mmol/L

83. Potassium (k) level in blood is

    a. 2.5-3.5 mmol/L

    b. 6.0-7.1 mmol/L

    c. 3.8-5.0 mmol/L

84. Blood cells in circulation are suspended in

    a. Gas

    b. Plasma

    c. Medication

85. The heaviest of the blood cells is

    a. Leukocytes

    b. Platelets

    c. Erythrocytes

86. The thin layer of whit substance formed on RBC after settling of blood is

   a. Buffy Coat

   b. Plasma

   c. Anticoagulants

87. Level of acidity and alkalinity of any solution is called

   a. PH

   b. OP

   c. SA

88. Normal range for lactic acid is

   a. 20-30 mg/dl

   b. 5-20   mg/dl

   c. 1-2 mg/dl

89. Range for normal triglycerides is

   a. 2-9 mg/dl

   b. 200-300 mg/dl

   c. 10-190 mg/dl

90. Serum is plasma without clotting factors

   a. True

   b. False

91. The process by which body stops bleeding vessel with platelet plug mesh work (clot) is called

    a. Homeostasis

    b. Hemostasis

    c. Hemoptysis

92. Coagulation phase is divided into two (2) main systems, namely

    a. Early and delayed

    b. Intrinsic and extrinsic

    c. fast and slow

93. _____ is inability of the heart to pump right amount of blood to the body because it cannot overcome vascular pressure characterized by tissue fluid excessive

    a. Congestive heart failure

    b. Hypertension

    c. Anemia

94. Condition where right side of the heart cannot function as expected due to disease in pulmonary pathology is

    a. convulsion

    b. emesis

    c. cor pulmonale

95. Restriction of blood supply in coronary arteries can result in

    a. headache

    b. myocardial infraction

    c. migraine

96. _____ ensues when blood supply to a part of brain is compromised

    a. cerebrovascular accident

    b. road traffic accident

    c. domestic accident

97. A weakness in wall of blood vessel resulting in swelling or balloon formation of the weakened wall is called

    a. Anemia

    b. Aneurysm

    c. Fatigue

98. Polycythemia mean

    a. Production of excessive RBC triggered by low O2 level

    b. Production of low RBC triggered by high O2 level

    c. Failure of body to Produce RBC at all

99. Increased leukocytes count because of infection is referred to

    A. Lymphoma

    B. Leukemia

C. Leukocytosis

100. A condition whereby erythrocytes and hemoglobin's are improperly formed due to inheritance is called

    A. Cardiac Arrest

    B. Analgesia

    C. Sickle cell anaemia

101. Excessive formation of nonfunctional and immature leukocytes is called

    A. Anaemia

    B. Leukemia

    C. Anorexia

102. A disorder in coagulation with prolonged clotting period is called

    A. Hemophilia

    B. Emphysema

    C. Hemolysis

103. _____is inflammation of the lymph vessel

    A. Osteomyhtis

    B. Lymphagitis

    C. Lump

104. Accumulation of blood in the tissue resulting from blood leak due to trauma is called

A. Hypoxia

B. Embolus

C. Hematoma

105. A protein substance that is converted to fibrin clot during hemostasis is called

A. Vitamin C

B. Vitamin K

C. Fibrinogen

106. _____ is clear colorless fluid in the lymphatic vessel

A. saliva

B. Lymph

C. Gas

107. Lymphadenitis is

A. Inflammation of bladder

B. Inflammation of lymph vessel

C. Inflammation of lymph gland

108. Hemolysis is defined as

A. Blood transfusion

B. Blood destruction

C. Blood formation

109. Minimal haemorrhogil spot under the skin is called

A. Peteclige

B. Poisoning

C. Thrombin

110. The easiest bleeding to control comes from which of these vessels?

A. Artery

B. Aorta

C. Capillary

SECTION FIVE

1. One of these is not an equipment used in venipuncture

   a. Vacuum tube

   b. Tourniquet

   c. Ignition key

2. Blood samples can be collected from veins, arteries, skin puncture

   a. True

   b. False

3. The most direct and effective blood sample collecting technique is the use of evacuated tube(vacutainer)

   a. False

   b. True

4. Disposable gloves and needle disposal container are not needed in venipuncture

a. True

b. False

5. _____and _____ are considered in describing vacuum tube size to be used

    a. Year of sample collection and patients level of education

    b. Years of experience of health worker and patient

    c. Tube length, external diameter and amount of specimen

6. Royal blue tube are usually for

    a. Toxicology and nutritional status

    b. Glucose monitoring

    c. Ammonia

7. Green tube with lithium heparin are normally used for testing except

    a. Glucose and blood urea nitrogen

    b. Creatinine and electrolytes studies

    c. Blood smear using wright's stain

8. Light blue tubes are used to collect which sample

    a. Sample for apt/ pt

    b. Sample for glucose

    c. Sample for culture and sensitivity

9. _____ additive is added to light blue tubes

    a. Lithium heparin

b. EDTA

c. Sodium citrate

10. Preservatives in anticoagulants can extend life spam of erythrocytes after blood draw

a. True

b. False

11. The following are used as anticoagulants in blood samples, except

a. Heparin

b. EDTA

c. Sterile water

12. One of these is not true when using vacuum blood tubes

a. Vacuum determine that amount of blood to be collected

b. Erroneous result can occur with insufficient blood volume

c. Any amount of blood can be collected

13. Yellow- top tubes are normally used in collecting blood samples for

a. Toxicology

b. Culture

c. Glucose

14. Aseptic technique is recommended when collecting culture blood sample because

a. Sample can be contaminated by skin

b. Sample can be contaminated automatically

c. Any volume of specimen can be used

15. Tube without anticoagulant are usually

a. Light- blue topped tube

b. Red- topped tube

c. Royal- blue topped tube

16. Potassium can be released from platelets during clotting

a. False

b. True

17. Sodium heparin, ammonia heparin and lithium heparin are not used in green-

topped tubes

a. True

b. False

18. In order to avoid microclots EDTA bottles should be completely inverted

a. 2-3 times

b. 1-2 times

c. 8-10 times

19. Tubes with EDTA used for most hematology procedures eg CBC are

a. Purple(lavender) topped tube

b. Royal blue topped tube

c. Yellow topped tube

20. Blood bank collections make use of

    a. Purple- topped tubes

    b. Red topped tubes

    c. Pink topped tubes

21. Glycolytic inhibitors

    a. Prevent break down of glucose

    b. Promote break down of glucose

    c. It is a useless additive

22. Gray- topped tubes are used in collecting samples for

    a. Blood

    b. Glucose

    c. Saliva

23. Gray- topped tube with oxalate should not be used for hematology because

    a. Oxalate is neutral on cellular morphology

    b. Oxalates pressures cellular morphology

    c. Oxalates alters cellular morphology

24. Tan- topped tube are used for

    a. Lead testing

    b. Glucose testing

c. 2- hour postprandial test

25. Black- topped tube with EDTA are used for erythrocytes sedimentation rate (ESR)

   a. True

   b. False

26. Identify one that is not part of safety syringe

   a. Needle and hub

   b. Wrist watch and ring

   c. Barrel and plunger

27. _____ us the needles used for collecting donor units of blood

   a. 16-18 gauge

   b. 21-22 gauge

   c. 22-23 gauge

28. Specimen for laboratory assays are collected with

   a. 17- 18 gauge needle

   b. 16-18 gauge needle

   c. 21-22 gauge needle

29. In gauge measurement, the smaller the gauge, the larger the needle diameter

   a. True

   b. False

30. Needles for phlebotomy may not be sterile before use

a. False

b. True

31. Protective holder that gives immediate protection from used needle is

    a. Venipuncture needle hub

    b. Venipuncture needle plunger

    c. Venipuncture needle- pro

32. In vanish point blood collection tube holder

    a. Needle remains outside until it is dropped in container

    b. Needle is automatically retracted from the patient

    c. Needle is expected to be bent by health worker

33. Sarstedts monovette venous blood collection system has needle with holder that

    needs no prior assembly before use

    a. True

    b. False

34. A one- time- use only safety- engineered device(like venipuncture needle pro) has

    the following benefits, except

    a. Lowers risk of causing contaminated equipment

    b. It scares both patient and health care worker

    c. Prevent accidental needle stick

35. Identify the importance of examining needle tip before use on patient

a. Examination time helps patients to prepare for venipuncture

b. Prevention of harm to patient from blunt tip

c. Enough time is wasted on patient to the advantage of healthcare worker

36. Using bent or blunt needle on patient can lead to the following

a. Serious injury to the patient

b. Failure to collect blood

c. Teach patient to appreciate the fact the venipuncture is not easy

37. Identify the benefit of a multiple- sample needle in venipuncture

a. Reduces cost in health care facility

b. Permits multiple tube changes and leakage barrier

c. Reduces precious time wasted on one patient

38. Incompatible needle and syringes or holder can lead to

a. Blood leakage and exposure to others

b. Preanalytical test error

c. Unexpected sample clotting

39. The most commonly used intravenous device is needle because

a. It is easily found on market

b. Nobody dislikes butterfly

c. It can be used on patients who are difficult to stick by others

40. At what time should health care worker ensure the availability of sharp container

a. During blood collection procedure

b. Before starting procedure for blood collection

c. After completing blood collection

41. Approved colors for sharp containers one of the following

a. White or gray

b. Blue or green

c. Orange or red

42. Good sharp container should be easily punctured

a. True

b. False

43. Recommended sharp container should not permit leakage

a. True

b. False

44. Identify one that is not expected function of tourniquets in venipuncture

a. Assists in vein assessment

b. Reduction of venous return to the heart

c. Restriction of eternal blood supply

45. Tourniquet application exerts pressure which results in

a. Pooling of arterial blood

b. Pooling of venous blood

c. Pain in the arm

46. The challenge of using blood pressure cuff during venipuncture is

    a. Contamination of the cuff

    b. Regulation disallow use of cuff

    c. It wastes a lot of time

47. Pressure appropriate to provide blood barrier in venipuncture is achieved when

    tourniquet exerts

    a. Pressure higher than systolic pressure

    b. Pressure lower than diastolic pressure

    c. Pressure below systolic but higher than diastolic pressure

48. Laboratory test errors arising from prolonged tourniquet pressure can be

    prevented by

    a. Not using tourniquet at all

    b. Partial reduction of same venous pressure

    c. Applying tourniquet and releasing it immediately

49. Cross contamination through multiple- use tourniquet can be prevented using

    these approaches, except

    a. Air drying when contaminated

    b. Multiple wiping with 70% isopropyl alcohol

    c. Use of 1:1- chlorine bleach preparation if contaminated

50._____ is the name of instrument that can assist detecting vein

    a. Venoscope

    b. Stethoscope

    c. Thermometer

51. Gloves with taic powder with calcium are not recommended by health care worker

    for phlebotomy because

    a. Contamination can lower calcium value in sample

    b. Contamination can raise calcium value in sample

    c. Contamination can alter sample color

52. Which one is true about storage of gloves

    a. Ensure gloves in stock are used up before 1 year

    b. Gloves can be safely used after 6 months

    c. Do not use stored glove after 3 months

53. It is safe to reuse gloves on not more than 2 patients

    a. True

    b. False

54. Gloves can be washed in preparation for reuse with

    a. Chlorine bleach dilution of 1:10

    b. Bleach dilution of 1:20

    c. None of above

55. It is appropriate to store gloves under intense light

    a. False

    b. True

56. Gloves, like other equipment should be examined briefly before use to rule out

    manufacture error

    a. True

    b. False

57. All of the following are used to prevent exposure to latex allergy, except

    a. Use of oil- based cream before donning gloves

    b. Washing of hands immediately after contact with gloves

    c. Choice of non-latex gloves with non-infectious materials

58. Which one of these items is not appropriate for blood collection

    a. Cotton wool swabs

    b. Sterile gauze pad

    c. 70% isopropyl alcohol

59. Blood collection related anemia can be prevented by

    a. Venipuncture

    b. Skin puncture

    c. Arterial blood collection

60. Penetrating bone at the heel of an infant during skin puncture is prevented by

a. Not exceeding 2-5 mm depth in penetration

b. Not exceeding 0- 1mm depth in penetration

c. Not exceeding 1-9 mm depth in penetration

61. During skin puncture at the heel_____ is the bone at risk of being penetrated

a. Calcaneus

b. Tibia

c. Fibula

62. Arm rest of blood- drawing chair should _____

a. Always be removed before venipuncture

b. Be static and not adjustable

c. Be adjusted up and down during venipuncture

63. Identify one of the following that is not a function of blood- collection armpit

a. Helps in accessing both arms of the patient

b. Serving as receptacle for blood leakage at all times

c. Provision of safety for patient

64. _____can be an option whenever blood- collection chair is not available

a. Examination table

b. Patient standing erect with support

c. None of the above

65. Specimen collection tray should be

a. Made of materials that can be sterilized

b. Made with breakable plates

c. Highly porous whenever there is specimen spill

66. Armrest of blood- collecting chair is made to lock in a place to

a. Easily fall off with patient if he faints

b. Prevent unwanted person from accessing the chair

c. Prevent patient from falling of chair if he faints

67. Latex- free blood collecting specimen tray is preferred to other materials

a. True

b. False

68. Collected blood must by transported with

a. Enclosed container

b. Open container

c. Perforated container

69. Biohazard symbol is not necessary on the container of transporting blood specimen

a. True

b. False

70. A locked specimen container serves the following purpose, except

a. Risk of contamination is highly reduced

b. It creates unnecessary suspicion

c. Specimen cannot be tampered with

71. Identify what can be done to prevent spills when transporting specimen

   a. Arrange for security escort

   b. Ensure tight seal

   c. Pix postal stamp on each container

72. Micro collection supplies are very important when working on which set of patients

   a. Children

   b. Young men

   c. Young women

73. Which one of these is not needed on specimen collection tray

   a. Disposable gloves

   b. Sterile gauze

   c. Surgical gloves

74. Identify the one not needed for skin preparation prior blood specimen collection

   a. 70% isopropyl

   b. Chlehexidine swabs

   c. Water soaked swabs

75. Biohazard waste container for used supplies are not necessary when working on children

   a. True

b. False

76.Which of these is not required on blood specimen collection tray

    a. Warming device

    b. Safety syringes

    c. None of the above

77.Safety lancet can be used for venipuncture

    a. True

    b. False

78.Identify the light- sensitive substance among the following

    a. Bilirubin

    b. Calcium

    c. Phosphorus

79._____ is the indication for color coding in needles packaging

    a. Gauge

    b. Company's name

    c. Anticoagulant

80.Identify the needle gauge with largest diameter

    a. 23

    b. 21

    c. 19

81. Glycolysis means

    a. Glucose build- up

    b. Glucose break down

    c. None of the above

82. Lavender(purple) topped tube is the appropriate for

    a. Blood culture in microbiology

    b. Most haematology such as complete blood count(CBC)

    c. Fasting blood sugar

83. The smaller the number of a needle gauge,

    a. The higher the flow rate

    b. The smaller the flow rate

    c. No flow rate in smaller gauge needle

84. The larger the number of a needle gauge, the

    a. Larger diameter of the needle

    b. The longer the length of the needle

    c. Smaller diameter of the needle

85. When the gauge of a needle is larger the flow rate will be

    a. Smaller

    b. Larger

    c. Extra- large

86. Best description for butterfly needle is

   a. One which butterfly is permitted to fly

   b. Needle used to kill butterfly in health facility

   c. Most frequently used winged infusion set

87. Sodium fluoride

   a. Inhibits destruction of glucose

   b. Promotes destruction of glucose

   c. Is not required in any of specimen tubes

88. _____ is found in green- topped tubes

   a. EDTA

   b. Amonium heparin

   c. Sodium fluoride

89. Anticoagulant may not be present in

   a. Purple- topped tubes

   b. Green- topped tubes

   c. Red- topped tubes

90. Hypoallergenic latex gloves lowers occurrence of latex allergy

   a. True

   b. False

91. Health care workers can protect himself from latex allergy by doing all of the following, except

    a. Prompt cleaning of contamination laden with latex dust

    b. Participate in latex health- education program

    c. Staying off- duty for 2 days after using latex gloves

92. Healthcare worker is permitted to patients without changing gloves if he has double gloves

    a. True

    b. False

93. Surgical blade can be carefully used for skin puncture

    a. True

    b. False

94. Collecting least volume of needed blood from patient

    a. Reduces the occurrence of induced anemia

    b. Reduces the time used on specimen

    c. Reduces the cost of laboratory tests

95. Pooling of venous blood with application of tourniquet

    a. Often leads to irreparable tourniquet damage

    b. Makes vein to be less visible

    c. Makes vein to be easily seen and feet

96. Skin puncture needs as much skin preparation as venipuncture

   a. True

   b. False

97. Enzymes in blood samples can be destroyed by which of these additives

   a. Lithium heparin

   b. Ethylenediaminetetraacetic Acid(EDTA)

   c. Sodium fluoride

98. EDTA- containing tubes used in blood bank samples should be inverted for how

   many times

   a. 3-4 times

   b. 8-10 times

   c. 15-20 times

99. Blood accumulation in the tissue as a result of traumatic leak is

   a. Hematoma

   b. Hemesis

   c. Homeostasis

100. Which of these is specifically important in arresting bleeding

   A. vitamin K

   B. Vitamin B12

   C. Vitamin C

SECTION SIX

1. Venesection means

A. Cutting the nerve

B. Cutting the capillary

C. Cutting the artery

D. Cutting the vein

2. Latin word vena means

   A. Artery

   B. Vein

   C. Nerve

   D. Capillary

3. Venesection is another word for

   A. Phlebotomy

   B. Apparatus

   C. Venipuncture

   D. Cupping

4. _____ comes from the Greek word

   A. Phlegm

   B. Hirudo

   C. Phlebos

D. Kinesics

5. What is thought to have contributed to George Washington death in 1799

   A. Excessive leeching

   B. Excessive cupping

   C. Excessive spooning

   D. Excessive phlebotomy

6. Early leech jars were glass and later ones are

   A. Ceramic

   B. Tile

   C. Wood

   D. Vinyl

7. _____ is used for more localized bloodletting

   A. Worms

   B. Snails

   C. Blades

   D. Leeches

8. Phlebotomy is preferred to

   A. Obtain blood for diagnostic purposes

   B. Remove blood for transfusions at a donor center

   C. Remove blood for therapeutic purposes

   D. All of the above

9. Venipuncture involves

    A. Collecting blood by tapping a vein with a pin and syringe or other collection apparatus

    B. Collecting blood by penetrating a vein with a needle and syringe or other collection apparatus

    C. Collecting blood by tapping a vein with the tip of a knife and syringe or other collection apparatus

    D. Collecting blood by penetrating a vein with a hammer and syringe or other collection apparatus

10. _____ involves collecting blood after puncturing the skin with a lancet

    A. Capillary puncture

    B. Acupuncture

    C. Mini puncture

    D. Venipuncture

11. Duties and responsibilities of a phlebotomist involves all of the following except

    A. Maintain safe working conditions

    B. Transport specimen to the laboratory

    C. Turning patient q 2 hours

    D. Perform skin tests

12. Which of the following is a voluntary process by which an agency grants recognition to an individual who has met certain prerequisites in a particular area

A. License

B. Continuing education

C. Certification

D. Professional

13. _____ is an act of granting a license

A. Licensure

B. Certificate

C. Professionalism

D. Continuing education

14. Which of the following state offers three levels of phlebotomy licensure

A. New York

B. Arizona

C. Las Vegas

D. California

15. Professionalism is defined as

A. The conduct and qualities that characterize a professional person

B. The conduct and issues that characterize a professional person

C. The product and qualities that characterize a professional person

16. The more _____ you have the more professional you appear

A. Self-awareness

B. Self-confidence

C. Self-actualization

D. Self-esteem

17. A phlebotomist often functions _____ and may be tempted to take procedural

short cuts when pressed for time

A. Dependently

B. Dependent

C. Professionally

D. Independently

18. Which of the following has to do with personal feeling of "wholeness"

A. Integrity

B. Disability

C. Diversity

D. Prosperity

19. _____ means being sensitive to a person's need and willing to offer

reassurance in a caring and humane way

A. Integrity

B. Confidentiality

C. Compassion

D. Dependability

20. Some personal behaviors and characteristics that make up professionalism include

all of the following except

A. Ethical behavior

B. Compassion

C. Self confidence

D. Sympathy

21. Which of the following include the phrase primum non nocere

A. Hippocratic oath

B. Patients' rights

C. HIPAA oath

D. Professionalism

22. Who publishes and disseminates a statement of patient rights and responsibilities

A. HIPPA

B. National Healthcare Association (NHA)

C. American Hospital Association (AHA)

D. CDC

23. All of the following is expected during hospital stay except

A. A clean and safe environment

B. A dirty and unsafe environment

C. Help when leaving the hospital

D. High quality hospital care

24. The acronym HIPAA means

A. Patient health information

B. Health information printing association

C. Health insurance portable accounting

D. Health Insurance Portability and accountability Act

25. Which of the following is the means by which information is exchanged or transmitted

A. Listening

B. Empathy

C. Sympathy

D. Communication

26. Which of the following is the three components of communication

A. Scratching, spitting and biting

B. Verbal skills, nonverbal skills and the ability to listen

C. Verbal skills, spitting and biting

D. Ability to listen, scratching and nonverbal skills

27. The most obvious form of communication is through _____ words

A. Written

B. Spoken

C. Expression

D. Facial expression

28. Which of the following are examples of communication barriers

A. Dependability

B. Compassion

C. Language limitations, cultural diversity, emotions, age and hearing loss

D. Self-confidence

Match the following going from top left to right

29. ___   happy

30. ___ , ___   surprise

31. ___ , ___   anger

32. ___   disgust

33. ___   fear

34. ___ , ___   sad

35. The study of nonverbal communication is also called

A. Kinesics

B. Kinect

C. Kinecta

D. Kinetic

36. When verbal and nonverbal messages do not match it is called

A. Kinecta

B. Kinesics

C. Kinesic slip

D. Kinetic

37. Personal zone radius is

A. 4 to 12 feet

B. 1 and 1/2 to 4 feet

C. More than 12 feet

D. Less than 2 feet

38. Intimate zone radius is

A. 3 feet

B. 6 to 8 feet

C. 12 inches

D. 1 to 18 inches

39. Proxemics is the study of

A. An individual's thoughts and use of language

B. An individual's mind and thinking

C. An individual's space and surroundings

D. An individual's concept and use of space

40. Empathy is defined as

A. A sense of well-being

B. Identifying with the feelings or thoughts of another person

C. Control of intimate zone

D. How thoughtful and sensitive people are

41. _____ is shown in both positive feeling for a person and in specific action demonstrating that positive feeling

A. Respect

B. Control

C. Touch

D. Empathy

42. What are the two general categories of healthcare facilities?

 A. Outpatient and temporary patient

B. Outpatient and inpatient

C. Transfer patient and temporary patient

D. Incontinent patient and inpatient

43. The abbreviation ICD-9-CM means

A. International Classification of Diseases, 10th rev., Clinical Modification

B. International Classification of Diseases, 19th rev., Clinical Modification

C. International Classification of Diseases, 10th rev., Procedural Coding System

D. International Classification of Diseases, 9th rev., Clinical Modification

44. The current procedural terminology (CPT) codes were originally developed in the

A. 1960s

B. 1950s

C. 1970s

D. 1980s

45. Which state is the only state that has devised its own system outside of Medicaid called the Arizona Health Care Cost Containment System (AHCCCS)

A. Arizona

B. California

C. Texas

D. Oregon

46. What is the generic name for a payment system that attempts to manage cost, quality and access to health care

A. Managed care

B. Damage care

C. Healthcare

D. None of the above

47. The term hospital can be applied to any healthcare facility that has any of the following except

A. Organized medical staff

B. Not protecting patient information

C. 24-hour nursing service

D. Permanent inpatient beds

Match the following specialist on the left to the area of interest on the right

48. Cardiologist   A. Tumors

49. Dermatologist   B. Rheumatic diseases

50. Gerontologist   C. Diseases of the heart and blood vessels

51. Hematologist   D. Function of the lungs

52. Neurologist   A. Diseases and injuries of the skin

53. Oncologist   B. Mental illness

54. Otorhinolaryngologist C. Effects of aging

55. Psychiatrist   D. Disorders of the eye, ear, nose and throat

56. Pulmonologist   A. Disorders of the blood

57. Rheumatologist   B. Disorders of the brain

58. _____ is the study of the ability of blood to form and dissolve clots

A. Hematology

B. Hemoglobin

C. Coagulation

D. None of the above

59. Which of the following is the abbreviation of hematocrit

A. Hgb

B. Hct

C. Hmt

D. Hmc

60. Hgb is the abbreviation for

A. Hemoglobin

B. Hemoglobin

C. Hematoma

D. None of the above

61. Which of the following are the two major divisions in the clinical laboratory?

A. Medical analysis areas and anatomical and surgical pathology

B. Tissue analysis areas and clinical analysis areas

C. Clinical analysis areas and anatomical and surgical pathology

D. Pathological analysis areas and clinical analysis areas

62. The most common chemistry specimen is

A. Blood

B. Serum

C. Platelet

D. Hemoglobin

63. The term serology means the study of

A. Blood

B. Platelet

C. Serum

D. Hemoglobin

64. Blood gases (ABG) test is associated with what body system

A. Liver

B. Heart

C. Bone

D. Kidneys and lungs

65. Glucose test is associated with what body system

A. Pancreas

B. Heart

C. Kidney

D. Liver

66. Ammonia test is associated with what body system

A. Kidney

B. Heart

C. Liver

D. Bone

67. Creatine kinase (CK) test is associated with what body system

A. Heart or muscle

B. Pancreas

C. Skin

D. Adrenals

68. _____ is defined as the study of the microscopic structure of tissues

A. Microbiology

B. Dermatology

C. Immunology

D. Histology

69. Two of the most common diagnostic techniques in histology found in the laboratory are

A. Biopsy and CT scan

B. Blood culture and frozen section

C. Glucose and biopsy

D. Biopsy and frozen section

70. Cytology tests are concern with the structure of

A. Bone

B. Cells

C. Muscle

D. None of the above

71. Common microbiological test include all of the following except

A. Blood culture

B. Gram stain

C. Glucose

D. Occult blood

72. The Pap smear test is name after which of the following

A. Dr. George Patterson

B. Dr. George Pittengill

C. Dr. George N. Papanicolaou

D. Dr. George P. Papilloma

73. The duty of a phlebotomist is to

A. Collect drug screen

B. To perform personal hygiene

C. Perform compatibility testing

D. None of the above

74. The territorial social zone radius is

A. 4 to 12 feet

B. 1 to 18 inches

C. more than 12 feet

D. 1 ½ to 4 feet

75. A disorder involving the over production of red blood cells is called

A. Polycythemia

B. Erythrocyte

C. Phlebotomy

D. None of the above

SECTION SEVEN

1. One of the keys players in bringing quality assessment review techniques to

   healthcare is

   A. The Joint Commission

   B. The National Healthcare Association

   C. Public Health Service

   D. None of the above

2. All of the following is good laboratory practices except

   A. Be sure to properly identify the patient

   B. Inform the patient of any test preparation such as fasting, clean catch urines,

   etc.

   C. Mix components of different kits

   D. None of the above

3. _____ is a global, nonprofit, standards-developing organization

   with representatives from the profession, industry, and government.

   A. Clinical laboratory improvement amendments

   B. Clinical and laboratory standard institute

   C. American society for clinical pathology

   D. College of American pathologists

4. Patient identification is the most important aspect of

A. Data collection

B. Personal collection

C. Specimen collection

D. None of the above

5. _____ checks help ensure quality in testing

A. Alpha

B. Beta

C. Gamma

D. Delta

6. Documents that are used when counseling or suspension is necessary is called

A. Near miss report form

B. Performance improvement plan

C. Equipment check form

D. None of the above

7. Risk is defined as

A. The chance of gain or injury

B. The chance of win or lose

C. The chance of loss or injury

D. The chance of win or win

8. The most common civil action in healthcare are based on

A. Tort law

B. Sweet law

C. Sour law

D. Hot law

9. An act or threat causing another to be in fear of immediate battery is an

    A. Assault

    B. Fraud

    C. Invasion of privacy

    D. Breach of confidentiality

10. An intentional harmful or offensive touching of, or use of force on another

    person without consent or legal justification is

    A. Battery

    B. Assault

    C. Fraud

    D. Invasion of privacy

11. _____ is a deceitful practice or false portrayal of facts either by words or

    by conduct often done to obtain money or property

    A. Invasion of privacy

    B. Fraud

    C. Malpractice

    D. Statute of limitation

12. The violation of one's right to be left alone is

A. Invasion of privacy

B. Implied consent

C. Assault

D. Battery

13. The failure to keep privileged medical information private

A. Battery

B. Assault

C. Breach of confidentiality

D. Fraud

14. A type of negligence committed by a professional

A. Respondent superior

B. Malpractice

C. Tort

D. Assault

15. Doing something that a reasonable person would not do

A. Assault

B. Res ipsa loquitur

C. Malpractice

D. Negligence

16. To claim negligence which of the following must be present

A. A legal duty or obligation owed by one person to another

B. A breaking or breach of that duty or obligation

C. Harm done as a direct result of the action

D. All of the above

17. A Latin phrase meaning "let the master respond"

A. Res ipsa loquitur

B. Torsades de pointes

C. Pointes res loquitur

D. Torsades ipsa res

18. A Latin phrase meaning "let the master respond"

A. Torsades de pointes

B. Pointes res loquitur

C. Respondeat superior

D. None of the above

19. The standard of care expected of everyone at all times

A. Patient care

B. Standard of care

C. Limited care

D. Total care

20. A law setting the length of time after an alleged injury in which the injured

person is permitted to file a lawsuit

A. Statute of limitations

B. Implied consent

C. Expressed consent

D. None of the above

21. Liability imposed by law on one person for acts committed by another is

A. Limited liability

B. Vicarious liability

C. Malpractice liability

D. Vicious liability

22. Which of the following is not a type of patient consent

A. HIV consent

B. Consent for minors

C. Expressed consent

D. Smiling consent

23. Malpractice litigation involve all of the following except

A. Phase five

B. Phase one

C. Phase two

D. Phase three

24. Outcomes are monitored by

A. A QG program

B. A QS program

C. A QQ program

D. A QA program

25. Established policies and procedures fall under an overall process called

    A. Quality equivalent (QE)

    B. Quality assurance (QA)

    C. Quality qualification (QQ)

    D. Quality sophistication (QS)

26. The use of checks and controls is called _____ _____

    A. Quality equivalent (QE)

    B. Quality qualification (QQ)

    C. Quality sophistication (QS)

    D. Quality control (QC)

27. The _____ manual contains procedures related to chemical, electrical, fire

    and radiation safety

    A. Procedure

    B. Infection control

    C. Specimen

    D. Safety

28. _____ _____ is an internal process focused on identifying and

    minimizing situations that pose risk to patients and employees

    A. Safety management

B. Fall management

C. Risk management

D. None of the above

29. The process used to settle legal disputes is called

A. Litigation

B. Negligence

C. Consent

D. Malpractice

30. The _____ is the oldest and largest healthcare standards-setting body in the nation

A. Community health accreditation program (CHAP)

B. Healthcare quality association on accreditation (HQAA)

C. Accreditation commission for health care (ACHC)

D. The Joint commission (TJC)

31. Jeopardizing a patient's care is the lack of a quality-control program for each area or specialty in the clinical laboratory services. This is an example of which of the following

A. Situational decision rules

B. Indirect impact standards requirements

C. Direct impact standards requirements

D. Immediate threat to health and safety

32. The lack of documentation for ongoing education of the staff is an example of

A. Indirect impact standards requirements

B. Direct impact standards requirements

C. Immediate threat to health and safety

D. Situational decision rules

33. Finding unlicensed personnel working in the facility in a state where licensure is required by law is an example of

A. Immediate threat to health and safety

B. Direct impact standards requirements

C. Indirect impact standards requirements

D. Situational decision rules

34. A blood bank refrigerator temperature out of range or serious problems with specimen labeling is an example of

A. Situational decision rules

B. Immediate threat to health and safety

C. Indirect impact standards requirements

D. Direct impact standards requirements

35. Which of the following does sentinel event do

A. Signal the need for commitment

B. Signal the need for policy

C. Signal the need for immediate investigation and response

D. Signal the need for a visit

36. The Joint Commission reported in 1995 through 2005, _____ is listed as the leading factor in the root causes of sentinel events

    A. Communication

    B. Infection

    C. Medication

    D. Identification

37. Which of the following is not included in the 2010 National Patient Safety Goals (NPSGs)

    A. Identify patient correctly

    B. Improve staff communication

    C. Prevent infection

    D. All of the above is included

38. Which of the following are federal regulations passed by congress and administered by the Centers for Medicare and Medicaid Services (CMS)

    A. College of American Pathologists (CAP)

    B. Clinical and Laboratory Standards Institute (CLSI)

    C. Clinical Laboratory Improvement Amendments of 1988 (CLIA 88)

    D. National Accrediting Agency for Clinical Laboratory Sciences (NAACLS)

SECTION EIGHT

1. Which of the following is a condition that results when a microorganism is able to invade the body, multiply and cause injury or disease

    A. Influenza

    B. Bacteria

    C. Air borne

    D. Infection

2. Microbes include all of the following except

    A. Bacteria

    B. Fungus

    C. Fish

    D. Viruses

3. Microbes that are pathogenic (causing or productive of disease) are called

    A. Influenza

    B. Pathogens

    C. Fungus

    D. None of the above

4. Communicable means

    A. Able to spread from person to animal

    B. Able to spread from person to person

    C. Able to spread from vector to person

D. Able to spread from animal to vector

5. The term _____ applies to infections acquired in hospitals

   A. Nassuacomial

   B. Nasecomial

   C. Nosocomial

   D. Nasacomial

6. How many components are there in the chain of infection

   A. 5

   B. 4

   C. 7

   D. 6

7. The infectious agent is also called the _____

   A. Causative agent

   B. Means of transportation

   C. Portal of exit

   D. Mode of transmission

8. Which of the following is not include in the means of infection transmission

   A. Droplet

   B. Contact

   C. Immunity

   D. Airborne

9. A physical transfer of an infectious agent to a susceptible host through close or intimate contact such as kissing is called

   A. Airborne transmission

   B. Direct contact transmission

   C. Vehicle contact transmission

   D. None of the above

10. _____ contact transmission can occur when a susceptible host touches contaminated objects such as patient bed linens, clothing, dressings, and eating utensils

   A. Airborne

   B. Direct

   C. Indirect

   D. Vehicle

11. Which of the following is the transmission of an infectious agent through contaminated food, water or drugs

   A. Vehicle transmission

   B. Droplet transmission

   C. Vector transmission

   D. All of the above

12. The transfer of an infectious agent to the mucous membranes of the mouth, nose or conjunctiva of the eyes of a susceptible individual is

A. Vehicle transmission

B. Car transmission

C. Vector transmission

D. Droplet transmission

13. Inanimate objects that can harbor material containing infectious agents are called

A. Fomites

B. Salmonella

C. Termites

D. Formats

14. A _____ is someone with a decreased ability to resist infection

A. Revertible host

B. Susceptible host

C. Infectious host

D. None of the above

15. Which of the following is not a way to break the chain of infection

A. Isolated procedures

B. Effective hand hygiene procedures

C. Keep the victim warm

D. Insect and rodent control

16. A microorganism that primarily infects individuals with weakened immune

systems is called an

A. Apportunist

B. Opportunist

C. Appertunist

D. Droplet transmission

17. Which of the following requires every healthcare institution to have an infection-control program responsible for protecting patients, employees, visitors and anyone doing business within the healthcare institutions from infection

A. Occupational safety and health administration (OSHA)

B. National fire protection association (NFPA)

C. National healthcare association (NHA)

D. Joint commission

18. Which of the following situations require hand hygiene procedures

A. Before and after going to the restroom

B. Before leaving the laboratory

C. Before going to lunch or on a break

D. All of the above

19. _____ recommend the use of alcohol-based antiseptic hand cleaners in place of hand washing as long as the hands are not visibly soiled

A. CDC/HICPAC

B. PPE

C. AHA

D. HCV

20. Personal protective equipment (PPE) provides a barrier against

    A. Airborne infection

    B. Infection

    C. Upper respiratory infection

    D. None of the above

21. One way in which an infection-control program minimizes the spread of infection

    is through the establishment of _____

    A. Personal procedure

    B. Protective procedure

    C. Reverse procedure

    D. Isolation procedure

22. _____ is used for patients who are highly susceptible to infections

    A. Protective/reverse isolation

    B. Standard isolation

    C. Universal isolation

    D. System isolation

23. Which of the following is a type of white blood cell

    A. Erythrocyte

    B. Microsite

    C. Neutrophil

D. Nanotrophil

24._____ are to be used for patients known or suspected to be infected or

colonized with highly transmissible or epidemiologically significant pathogens

A. Biosafety

B. Percutaneous

C. Transmission precaution

D. Airborne precautions

25._____ must be used in addition to standard precautions for patients

known or suspected to be infected with microorganisms transmitted by airborne

droplet nuclei

A. Biosafety

B. Transmission precaution

C. Airborne precautions

D. Standard precautions

26._____ must be used in addition to standard precautions for patients

known or suspected to be infected with microorganisms transmitted by droplets

(when patient talk, coughs, sneezes etc.)

A. Droplet precautions

B. Universal precautions

C. Airborne precautions

D. Contact precautions

27. _____ must be used in addition to standard precautions when a patient is known or suspected to be infected with epidemiologically important microorganisms that can be transmitted by direct contact

A. Droplet precautions

B. Universal precautions

C. Airborne precautions

D. Contact precautions

28. _____ is the term used to describe the safe handling of biological substances that pose a risk to health

A. Biohazard

B. Biosafety

C. Droplet

D. Contact precautions

29. Anything harmful or potentially harmful to health is called a _____ and should be identified by a _____

A. Biosafety

B. Biochemical

C. Transmission

D. Biohazard, biohazard symbol

30. Ingestion is probably the most easily recognized, but routes other than the digestive tract referred to as _____

    A. Potentials

    B. Percutaneous

    C. Parental

    D. None of the above

31. Patients with airborne diseases can transmit infection to workers unless _____ respirator are worn when caring for them

    A. N98

    B. N95

    C. N97

    D. N96

32. _____ exposure to bio hazardous microorganisms in blood or body fluids occurs through intact skin

    A. Permucosal

    B. Percutaneous

    C. Parental

    D. Biohazard

33. _____ exposure occurs when infectious microorganisms and other biohazards enter the body through the mucus membranes of the mouth and nose

    A. Permucosal

B. Percutaneous

C. Parental

D. Biohazard

34. The term _____ is applied to any in

A. Airborne pathogen

B. Blood-borne pathogen

C. Parental pathogen

D. Bony pathogen

35. Hepatitis B is caused by

A. HIV

B. HBV

C. HCV

D. HVC

36. Hepatitis means

A. Inflammation of the liver

B. Inflammation of the gallbladder

C. Inflammation of the kidneys

D. Inflammation of the pancreas

37. _____ can be present in blood and other body fluids such as urine, semen, saliva etc.

A. HBV

B. HC

C. HTC

D. None of the above

38. What is the most widespread chronic blood-borne illness in the United States

A. Hepatitis A

B. Hepatitis D

C. Hepatitis E

D. Hepatitis C

39. Which of the following is found primarily in blood and serum, less frequently in saliva

A. HNV

B. HTV

C. HFV

D. HCV

40. HIV attacks the body's _____ system

A. Immune

B. Circulatory

C. Lymph

D. Nervous

41. During this phase the virus enters the T lymphocytes, triggering them to produce multiple copies of the virus

A. Incubation phase

B. Final phase

C. Active phase

D. None of the above

42. In this phase the virus hides in the T lymphs

A. Incubation phase

B. Inactive incubation phase

C. Final phase

D. Fourth phase

43. _____ are devices that isolate or remove a blood-borne pathogen

A. House controls

B. Blood controls

C. Engineering controls

D. Standard controls

44. The blood-borne pathogen standard was revised in _____ to conform to the needle stick safety and prevention act

A. 1991

B. 2003

C. 2000

D. 2001

45. OSHA requires surfaces in specimen collection and processing areas to be decontaminated by cleaning them with a 1:10 bleach solution or other disinfectant approved by the

A. Environmental policy act

B. Environmental protection agency (EPA)

C. Environmental policy holder

D. Environmental policy allowance

46. How many classes of fire are now recognized by the National Fire Protection Association (NFPA)

A. Four

B. Five

C. Three

D. Two

47. Fires that occur with ordinary combustible materials

A. Class A

B. Class D

C. Class K

D. Class B

48. _____ fires that occur with flammable liquids

A. Class A

B. Class D

C. Class K

D. Class B

49._____ are electrical fires

A. Class A

B. Class C

C. Class D

D. Class K

50._____ fires occur with combustible or reactive metals

A. Class A

B. Class C

C. Class D

D. Class K

51._____ fires occur with high-temperature cooking oils, grease, fats and

require agents that prevent splashing and cooling the fire as well as smother it

A. Class B

B. Class D

C. Class K

D. Class A

52.___ Class A extinguishers   A. use potassium-based alkaline liquid

53.___ Class B extinguishers   B. use dry chemical reagents to smother fire

54.___ Class C extinguishers   C. use soda and acid or water to cool the fire

55.___ Class ABC extinguishers D. use foam, dry chemical or carbon dioxide to smother

56.___ Class K extinguishers   A. use dry chemical, carbon dioxide, Halo or other …..

57. The acronym RACE means

A. Require, alarm, confine, extinguish

B. Rescue, alert, confine, extinguish

C. Rescue, alarm, confine, extinguish

D. None of the above

58. OSHA developed the _____ _____ _____ to protect employees who may be exposed to hazardous chemicals

A. Hazards communication standard

B. Hazard communication standard

C. Hazard communion standard

D. None of the above

59. The United Nations hazard class 8 use the symbol of a

A. Test tube over hand

B. Slashed

C. Flame

D. Bursting ball

60. All of the following are examples of the United Nations hazard class 5 except

A. Ammonium nitrate

B. Benzoyl peroxide

C. Calcium chlorite

D. Dynamite

61. The united Nations hazard class 1 background color is

A. Red

B. Yellow

C. Orange

D. Green

62. Which of the following is not an example of the United Nations class 7

A. Cobalt 14

B. Plutonium

C. Gasoline

D. Uranium

63. What is the symbol of the United Nations hazard class 3

A. Cylinder

B. Bursting ball

C. Slashed W

D. Flame

64. Think of the letters _____ to remember the safety rule always add acid

A. AAA

B. ABC

C. ACG

D. AGA

65. The National Fire Protection Association (NFPA) indicate health hazards with a

A. Red diamond in upper quadrant

B. Blue diamond on the left

C. Yellow diamond on the right

D. White quadrant on the bottom

66. The National Fire Protection Association (NFPA) indicated specific hazards in a

A. Yellow diamond on the right

B. White quadrant on the bottom

C. White quadrant on the top

D. None of the above

67. _____ is tearing away or amputation of a body part

A. Avulsion

B. Evaluation

C. Quadrant

D. Compression

68. Common symptoms of shock include all of the following except

A. Increase shallow breathing rate

B. Keep the victim warm until help arrive

C. Pale, cold, clammy skin

D. Expressionless face and staring eyes

69. All of the following involve providing first aid to a victim of shock except

    A. Call for assistance

    B. Use the defibrillator

    C. Maintain an open airway for the victim

    D. Keep the victim warm until

70. The phlebotomy programs require this course as a prerequisite

    A. ACLS

    B. PALS

    C. CPR/BLS

    D. None of the above

71. BLS single rescuer compression-to-ventilation ratio stays at

    A. 30:2

    B. 15:2

    C. 32:2

    D. 30:15

72. AHA links in the chain of survival include which of the following

    A. Rapid defibrillation

    B. Immediate recognition of cardiac arrest

    C. Effective advance life support

D. All of the above

73. Personal wellness requires a _____ approach

    A. Holistic

    B. Spiritual

    C. Holy

    D. Social

74. A healthy diet provide a good balance of all of the following except

    A. Protein

    B. Fiber

    C. Sugar

    D. Vitamins

75. The most accurate measurements of fitness consist of three components what are

    they

    A. Strength

    B. Flexibility

    C. Endurance

    D. All of the above

76. _____ is a form of exercise that can easily be incorporated into almost

    anyone's life

    A. Walking

    B. Jogging

C. Talking

D. Skipping

77. Yoga and pilates are two forms of exercise that emphasize

A. Bending, stretching and twisting

B. Conditioning or exercise

C. Excellent strength exercise

D. None of the above

78. The _____ is designed to withstand everyday movement

A. Spine

B. Muscle

C. Thighs

D. Hands

79. _____ is condition or state that results when physical, chemical, or

emotional factors cause mental or bodily

A. Exhaustion

B. Bored

C. Ulcers

D. Stress

80. Pathogenic means

A. Growing disease

B. Adding disease

C. Causing or productive of disease

D. Becoming a disease

81. There are _____ many links in the chain of infection

   A. 3

   B. 6

   C. 4

   D. 5

82. The source of infectious agent is called a _____

   A. Susceptible host

   B. Reservoir

   C. Infectious agent

   D. None of the above

83. Reservoirs include which of the following

   A. Humans

   B. Animals

   C. Food

   D. All of the above

84. A _____ is a way an infectious agent is able to leave a reservoir host

A. Entry pathway

B. Exit pathway

C. Vehicle

D. Contact

85. Means of transmission does not include which of the following

   A. Airborne, contact

   B. Droplet, vector

   C. Vector, vehicle

   D. All of the above

86. Which of the following is the most important means of preventing the spread of

   infection provided that it is achieved properly and when required

   A. Foot hygiene

   B. Teeth hygiene

   C. Hand hygiene

   D. Face hygiene

87. Microbiocidal means

   A. Destructive to microbes

   B. Destructive to fungus

   C. Destructive to virus

   D. Destructive to plants

88. After the use of gloves they should be

   A. Removed promptly in an aseptic manner and discarded

   B. Kept to be used again

   C. Placed in pocket of healthcare worker until they are ready to discard them

D. Kept for a count

SECTION NINE

1. A word _____ is the subject of a medical term and the foundation upon which the
   term is built

   A. Branch

   B. Stem

   C. Root

   D. Trunk

2. The word thrombophlebitis mean

   A. Fat

   B. Blood

   C. Clot

   D. Inflammation

3. A _____ is a word element that comes before a word root

   A. Suffix

   B. Root

   C. Stem

   D. Prefix

4. A _____ is a word ending

A. Suffix

B. Root

C. Stem

D. Prefix

5. The prefix a means

A. Without

B. Within

C. With end

D. Birth

Match the following root and their meaning

6. _____ Adip   A. vein

7. _____ Arteri   B. hard

8. _____ Cutane   C. death

9. _____ Enter   D. form

10._____ Hem   A. tissue

11._____ Hist   B. blood

12._____ Morph   C. intestines

13._____ Necr   D. skin

14._____ Scler   A. artery

15._____ Ven   B. fat

Match the following prefix and their meaning

16._____ Aniso   A. rapid

17._____ Ab   B. below, under

18._____ Brady   C. new

19._____ Dys   D. small

20._____ Extra   A. equal, same

21._____ Iso   B. outside

22._____ Micro   C. difficult

23._____ Neo   D. slow

24._____ Sub   A. unequal

25._____ Tachy   B. away from

26.A _____ is a vowel that is added between two word roots

   A. Binding vowel

   B. Nonbinding vowel

   C. Combining vowel

   D. None of the above

Match the following medical suffixes and their meaning

   27._____ –algia   A. small

   28._____ –centesis   B. stopping, controlling, standing

   29._____ –ism   C. breathing

   30._____ - rhage   D. oxygen level

   31._____ _ lysis   A. enlargement

32._____ - megaly B. breakdown, destruction

33._____ -oxia C. bursting forth

34._____ -pnea D. state of

35._____ -stasis A. surgical puncture to remove a fluid

36._____ -ule B. pain

Match the abbreviation to the meaning

37._____ ABGs A. biopsy

38._____ ACTH B. albumin

39._____ alb C. acute myelocytic leukemia

40._____ AML D. antistreptolysin O

41._____ ASO A. blood urea nitrogen

42._____ BUN B. arterial blood gases

43._____ Bx C. computed axial tomography

44._____ CAT D. creatine kinase

45._____ CK A. chronic myelogenous leukemia

46._____ CML B. adrenocorticotropic hormone

Match the abbreviation to their meaning

47._____ C-section A. sinoatrial

48._____ D B. rule out

49._____ DNA C. right

50._____ ECG D. prostrate specific antigen

51._____ EMG   A. partial thromboplastin time

52._____ ETOH   B. purified protein derivation (TB test)

53._____ FH   C. orally (per os)

54._____ GH   D. hydrogen ion concentration

55._____ GYN   A. pathology

56._____ HBV   B. operating room

57._____ HGB/hgb C. nonsteroidal anti-inflammator drug

58._____ h/o   D. negative

59._____ ID   A. milliliter

60._____ Kg   B. microgram

61._____ LDL   C. electrolytes

62._____ lytes   D. low-density lipoprotein

63._____ Mcg   A. kilogram

64._____ ML   B. identification, intradermal

65._____ Neg   C. history of

66._____ NDAID   D. hemoglobin

67._____ OR   A. hepatitis b virus

68._____ Path   B. gynecology

69._____ pH   C. growth hormone

70._____ p.o   D. family history

71._____ PPD   A. ethyl alcohol

72._____ PTT   B. electromyogram

73._____ PSA   C. electrocardiogram

74._____ R   D. deoxyribonucleic acid

75._____ R/O   A. day

76._____ SA   B. cesarean section

77. Segmented white blood cells are abbreviated as

    A. Segs

    B. SLE

    C. Sed rate

    D. SWBC

78. Which of the following is the abbreviation of systemic lupus erythematosus

    A. SLE

    B. Segs

    C. Sed rate

    D. SWBC

79. Sol is the abbreviation for

    A. Symptoms

    B. Subcutaneous

    C. Segmented white blood cells

    D. Solution

80. SpGr means

A. Serum glutamic-oxaloacetic transaminase

B. Specific gravity

C. Solution

D. Staphylococcus

81. Sx is the abbreviation for which of the following

A. Solution

B. Specific gravity

C. Symptoms

D. Subcutaneous

82. TIA mean

A. Temperature, pulse and respiration

B. Total iron binding capacity

C. Thyroid-stimulating hormone

D. Transcient ischemic attack

83. Total iron binding capacity is abbreviated by which of the following

A. T&C

B. TPN

C. TPR

D. TIBC

84. Trig is the abbreviation for which of the following

A. Triglycerides

B. Trigon anomy

C. Thyroid-stimulating hormone

D. treatment

85._____ is abbreviation for thyroid-stimulating hormone

    A. TFH

    B. TSH

    C. TIH

    D. None of the above

86. Wound is abbreviated by which of the following

    A. Wu

    B. Ww

    C. Wt

    D. Wd

87. Which of the following is on The Joint Commission's "Do Not Use" List

    A. MS

    B. U

    C. IU

    D. All of the above

88. One of the following is on the Possible Future Additions to the "Do Not Use" List

    A. UTI

    B. VD

C. < (less than)

D. MS

89. Medical terminology is based on an understanding of which of the following

   A. Word roots

   B. Prefixes

   C. Suffixes

   D. All of the above

90. Modern medicine was founded by the _____ and influenced by _____

   A. Greeks, Latin

   B. Italian, Greeks

   C. Spanish, Latin

   D. None of the above

91. The root word cry means

   A. Cell

   B. Red

   C. Cold

   D. Child

92. The root word ped means

   A. Birth

   B. Hard

   C. Child

D. Death

93. Which of the following is an example of the root word cyan

    A. Coronary

    B. Cytology

    C. Cyanotic

    D. Child

94. The prefix homo means

    A. Different

    B. Unequal

    C. Equal

    D. Same

95. The prefix bio means

    A. Death

    B. Life

    C. Study of

    D. New

96. The prefix exo means

    A. Outside

    B. Inside

    C. Around

    D. Surround

97. The suffix –logy means

    A. Condition

    B. State or condition

    C. Study of

    D. State of

98. The suffix –spasm means

    A. Bursting forth

    B. Tumor

    C. Moving

    D. Twitch

99. The suffix –emia means

    A. State or condition

    B. Condition

    C. Formation

    D. Blood condition

100.   The suffix –penia means

    A. Disease

    B. Blood condition

    C. Deficiency

    D. Excision

101.   Phasia means

A. Small

B. Twitch

C. Speech

D. Rapid

102.   Aphasia means

A. Without speech

B. Speech

C. Twitch

D. Small

103.   The term ilium means

A. Neck bone

B. Hipbone

C. Thigh bone

D. Leg bone

104.   The term ileum means

A. Large intestine

B. Hipbone

C. Small intestine

D. Stomach

105.   The acronym CBC means

A. Coronary care unit

B. Complete blood count

C. Cubic centimeter

D. Chemotherapy

SECTION TEN

1. The human body is consist of over _____ cells

   A. 30 trillion cells

   B. 25 trillion

   C. 31 trillion

   D. 29 trillion

2. The human body is consist of approximately _____ of blood

   A. 15 liters

   B. 25 liters

   C. 7 liters

   D. 5 liters

3. A person in a _____ position is standing erect, arms at the sides with eyes and

   palms facing forward

   A. Anatomical

   B. Proximal

   C. Sagittal

D. None of the above

4. The act of turning the hand so that the palm faces down is called

   A. Transverse

   B. Supination

   C. Pronation

   D. Prone

5. The act of turning the palm to face upward is called

   A. Supination

   B. Soupination

   C. Suppernation

   D. Supination

6. A _____ plane is a flat surface resulting from a real or imaginary cut through a body in the normal anatomical position

   A. Frontal

   B. Body

   C. Sagittal

   D. Coronal

7. _____ plane divides the body vertically into front and back portions

   A. Frontal (coronal)

   B. Transverse

   C. Medial

D. Sagittal

8. Various organs of the body are housed in large, hollow spaces called

A. Anatomical cavities

B. Abdominal cavity

C. Body cavity

D. Ventral cavity

9. _____ is on or near the surface of the body

A. Anterior

B. Lateral

C. Superior

D. External (superficial)

10. Which of the following directional terms mean toward the midline or middle of the

body

A. Palmar

B. Inferior

C. Medial

D. Distal

11. _____ directional term mean nearest the center of the body, origin, point of

attachment

A. Proximal

B. Lateral

C. Distal

D. Internal

12. Which of the following directional terms mean within or near the center of the body

   A. Medial

   B. Internal (deep)

   C. External (superficial)

   D. Dorsal

13. _____ mean concerning the sole of the foot

   A. Palmar

   B. Dorsal

   C. Plantar

   D. Pelvic

14. This directional term is the farthest from the center of the body, origin or point of

   attachment

   A. Ventral

   B. External

   C. Palmar

   D. Distal

15. Which of the following cavities are located in the back of the body

   A. Pelvic

   B. Distal

C. Dorsal

D. Central

16._____ cavities are located in the front of the body

A. Boca

B. Medial

C. Ventral

D. Central

17. The thoracic cavity is separated from the abdominal cavity by a muscle called the

A. Balloon

B. Diaphragm

C. Bicep

D. Tricep

18. Homeostasis means

A. Bending the same

B. Standing the same

C. Skipping the same

D. Running the same

19._____ is the sum of all the physical and chemical reactions necessary to

sustain life

A. Cannibalism

B. Anabolism

C. Catabolism

D. Metabolism

20. Which of the following metabolism is a destructive process by which complex substances are broken down into simple substances, usually with the release of energy

A. Homeostasis

B. Catabolism

C. Spinal

D. None of the above

21. The _____ is the basic unit of all life

A. Cell

B. Cytoplasm

C. Chromosomes

D. Cilia

22. Which of the following component of cell encloses the cell and regulates what moves in and out of it

A. Peroxisomes

B. Lysosomes

C. Vesicles

D. Plasma membrane

23. The command center of the cell that contains the chromosomes or genetic material is called

A. Nucleus

B. Mitochondria

C. Golgi apparatus

D. Flagellum

24. Long strands of DNA organized into units called genes is known as

A. Surface organelles

B. Nucleolus

C. Endoplasmic reticulum (ER)

D. Nucleus

25. Which of the following is the function of the organelles

A. Move the cell or moves fluids around the cell

B. Varied, distinct functions depending on the type

C. Site of numerous cellular activities

D. Increase surface area for absorption

26. Which of the following components makes, sorts and prepares protein compounds for transport

A. Cytoplasm

B. Microvilli

C. Golgi apparatus

D. None of the above

27. This component is described as oval or rod-shaped organelles

   A. Microvilli

   B. Flagellum

   C. Nucleus

   D. Mitochondria

28. _____ are groups of similar cells that work together to perform a special

   function

   A. Muscles

   B. Organs

   C. Tissues

   D. None of the above

29. Which of the following is another name for fat

   A. Adipose

   B. Fascia

   C. Phalanx

   D. Cartilage

30. The _____ system is the framework that gives the body shape and support,

   protects internal organs and with the muscular system provides movement and

   leverage

   A. Skeletal

B. Muscular

C. Immune

D. Bone

31. The skeletal system is made up of _____ bones

    A. 200

    B. 201

    C. 206

    D. 209

32. Which of the following is the junction or union between two or more bones

    A. Bones

    B. Joint

    C. Muscle

    D. Fiber

33. Some joints have a small sac nearby called a

    A. Hematopoiesis

    B. Hemopoiesis

    C. Muscle

    D. Bursa

34. The back bones and some facial bones are examples of what bone shape

    A. Irregular

    B. Short

C. Flat

D. Long

35. Which of the following are examples of short bones

A. Wrist (carpals) and ankle bones (tarsals)

B. Rib bones and most skull bones

C. Leg arm and hand bones

D. None of the above

36. Abnormal growth of bone tissue is called

A. Rickets

B. Gout

C. Bone tumor

D. Osteomyelitis

37. _____ is disorder involving loss of bone density

A. Osteomyelitis

B. Osteoporosis

C. Osteochrondritis

D. Bursitis

38. Which of the following are the three types of muscles in the body

A. Cardiac

B. Skeletal

C. Smooth

D. All of the following

39. Integument means

    A. Muscle

    B. Ribs

    C. Teeth

    D. Covering or skin

40. The exocrine glands is also known as the

    A. Oil and sweat gland

    B. Hair and nails

    C. Sweat and heat

    D. Skin and sweat

41. Which of the following is the deepest layer of the epidermis

    A. Dermis

    B. Exocrine

    C. Stratum germminativum

    D. None of the above

42. The dermis is also called _____ or _____ is in the inner layer of the skin

    A. Conium

    B. Corium

    C. Basale

D. Keratinized

43. Muscle pain is also called

    A. Myalgia

    B. Atrophy

    C. Muscle dystrophy

    D. Tendonitis

44. Which of the following appendage is responsible for formation of "goose bumps" as they react to pull the hair up straight when a person is cold or frightened

    A. Nails

    B. Hair

    C. Sudoriferous

    D. Arrector pili

45. Which of the following skin disorder is elevated overgrowth of scar tissue at a wound or incision site

    A. Psoriasis

    B. Fungal infection

    C. Acne

    D. Keloid

46. The nervous system has _____ functional divisions

    A. Four

    B. Three

C. Two

D. Five

47. Which of the following functional nervous system division conduct impulses that allow an individual to consciously control skeletal muscles

A. Autonomic

B. Somatic

C. Ionic

D. Diagnostic

48. Neurons have a cell body containing a nucleus and organelles typical of other cells, but are distinguished by unique thread-like fibers called _____ and _____ that extend out from the cell body

A. Dendrites, ions

B. Dendrites, axons

C. Meninges, axons

D. Axons, neurons

49. The brain and spinal cord are surrounded by a cavity filled with a clear, plasma-like fluid called _____

A. Cerebrospinal fluid

B. Spinal fluid

C. Cell body fluid

D. CNS fluid

50. Which of the following nervous system disorders below is an acute eruption of herpes blisters along the course of a peripheral nerve

    A. Amyotrophic lateral sclerosis

    B. Shingles

    C. Neuralgia

    D. Meningitis

51. The word _____ comes from the Greek words endon, meaning "within" and Krinein meaning "to secrete"

    A. Endocrine

    B. Encephalitis

    C. Serotonin

    D. Peripheral nervous system

52. The _____ secrete erythropoietin (EPO), which stimulates red blood cell production when oxygen levels are low

    A. Heart

    B. Brain

    C. Skin

    D. kidney

53. Which of the following gland help set diurnal rhythm with levels lowest around noon and peaking at night

    A. Parathyroid

B. Pituitary

C. Pineal

D. Thymus

54. The gland islets of Langerhans produces _____ hormone

A. Melatonin

B. Testosterone

C. Calcitonin

D. Insulin

55. A condition characterized by anemia, slow speech, mental apathy, drowsiness, and sensitivity to cold resulting from decreased thyroid function is called

A. Myxedema

B. Acromegaly

C. Goiter

D. Dwarfism

56. A condition characterized by a swollen, "moon-shaped" face and redistribution of fat to the abdomen and back of the neck caused by an access of cortisone is called

A. Addison's disease

B. Cushing's syndrome

C. Aldosteronism

D. None of the above

57. Pregnancy tests are based on a reaction with a hormone called _____

_____ _____ secreted by embryonic cells that eventually give rise to the

placenta

    A. Human chorionic gonadotropin

    B. Hypersecretion

    C. Hyposecretion

    D. Glycosylated hemoglobin

58. Important digestive functions of the liver include which of the following

    A. Glycogen storage

    B. Detoxification of harmful substances

    C. Protein catabolism

    D. All of the above

59. Diverticulosis is

    A. Inflammation of the pancreas

    B. Inflammation of the liver

    C. Pouches in the walls of the colon

    D. Open sores or lesion

60. In males, the gametes are called

    A. Ovum

    B. Spermatozoa

    C. Ova

D. Ovary

61. The PAP smear, a procedure used to diagnose cervical cancer, is named after

    _____ _____ who developed the technique

    A. Greg Papanicolaou

    B. Gerod Papanicolaou

    C. George Papanicolaou

    D. Gregory Papanicolaou

62. Two chromosomes called _____ and _____ determine gender

    A. X, Y

    B. X, B

    C. Y, Z

    D. Y, E

63. Which of the following is not one of the main structures of the urinary system are

    A. Two renal artery

    B. Two kidneys

    C. Two ureters

    D. A urinary bladder and a urethra

64. The functional or basic unit of the kidney is the

    A. Ureter

    B. Nephron

    C. Glomerulus

D. Urethra

65. Nephritis is

A. Bladder inflammation

B. Inflammation of the kidneys

C. Impaired kidney function with a buildup of waste products in the blood

D. Sudden and severe impairment of renal function

66. The nose provide the main airway for _____ respiration

A. Internal

B. Super sternal

C. Lateral

D. External

67. Prolonged hyperventilation causes a decrease in carbon dioxide, resulting in an

increase in pH and a condition called

A. Alkalosis

B. Acidosis

C. Acidity

D. Alkalinity

68. The major respiratory tract structures include which of the following

A. Nose and pharynx

B. Larynx and trachea

C. Bronchi and lungs

D. All of the above

69. The _____ are tiny air sacs in the lungs where the exchange of oxygen and carbn dioxide takes place

    A. Capillary

    B. Bronchioles

    C. Pleura

    D. Alveoli

70. Apnea is

    A. Inflammation of the pleura membrane

    B. Difficulty or labored breathing

    C. A temporary cessation of breathing

    D. Infection of the tonsils

71. A deficiency of surfactant in premature infants causes the alveoli to collapse, leading to a condition called

A. Upper respiratory distress syndrome

B. Infant respiratory distress syndrome

C. Asthma

D. Bronchitis

72. Which of the following planes divides the body vertically into equal right and left portions

    A. Midsagittal (medial) plane

B. Frontal (coronal) plane

C. Sagittal plane

D. Transverse plane

73. Which of the following divides the body horizontally into upper and lower portions

A. Frontal (coronal) plane

B. Transverse plane

C. Sagittal plane

D. Midsagittal (medial) plane

74. Anterior (ventral) means

A. Toward the side of the body

B. To the back of the body

C. Toward the midline or middle of the body

D. To the front of the body

75. The directional term superior is paired with which of the following

A. Distal

B. Lateral

C. Inferior

D. Proximal

76. The directional term lateral means

A. To the back of the body

B. Nearest the center of the body

C. Toward the side of the body

D. To the front of the body

77. The directional term posterior is paired with which of the following

A. Superior

B. Medial

C. Proximal

D. Anterior

78. _____ is a constructive process by which the body converts simple compounds into complex substances needed to carry out the cellular activities of the body

A. Catabolism

B. Anabolism

C. Metabolism

D. None of the above

79. Which of the following component of the cell makes ribosomes

A. Centrioles

B. Nucleolus

C. Cilia

D. Ribosomes

80. The DNA doubles and the cell divides by a process called

A. Mitosis

B. Cytosis

C. Centrioles

D. None of the above

SECTION ELEVEN

1. The heart is a _____ hollow, muscular organ that is slightly larger than a

   man's' closed fist

   A. Four-chambered

   B. Five-chambered

   C. Two-chambered

   D. Three-chambered

2. The upper chamber on each side of the heart are called

   A. Ventricles

   B. Septa

   C. Septum

   D. Atria

3. Which of the following layer covers the heart and attaches to the pericardium

   A. Endocardium

   B. Epicardium

   C. Septum

D. Myocardium

4. The inner layer of the heart is known as

   A. Epicardium

   B. Myocardium

   C. Endocardium

   D. Septum

5. Semi luna is Latin for

   A. Full moon

   B. Quarter moon

   C. Big moon

   D. Half moon

6. This valve closes when the right ventricle relaxes and prevents blood from flowing
   back into the right ventricle

   A. Right semilunar or pulmonic valve

   B. Aortic valve

   C. Tricuspid valve

   D. Mitral valve

7. Myocardial infarction means

   A. Heart muscle

   B. Heart crown

   C. Heart attack

D. None of the above

8. The contracting phase of the cardiac cycle is called

   A. Diastole

   B. Ischemia

   C. Systole

   D. Septum

9. Which of the following structure below begins the heartbeat by generating the electrical pulse that travels through the muscles of both atria

   A. AV bundle

   B. Sinoatrial (SA) node

   C. Intermodal pathway fibers

   D. Bundle of his

10. The AV bundle (bundle of his) is located at the

    A. Upper wall of the right atrium

    B. Bottom of the right atrium

    C. Wall of the right atrium

    D. Top of the interventricular septum

11. An irregularity in the heart rhythm or beat is called an _____

    A. Fibrillation

    B. Arrhythmia

    C. Dysrhythmia

D. Murmurs

12._____ is the force or tension exerted by the blood on the walls of blood

vessels

A. Diastole

B. Heart rate

C. Blood pressure

D. Pulse

13.The America Heart Association defines normal blood pressure as less than _____

over _____ mm Hg

A. 110/80

B. 120/90

C. 120/80

D. 110/70

14.Pericarditis is

A. Narrowing of the aorta or its opening

B. An infection of the lining of the heart

C. Heart attack or death of heart muscle

D. Inflammation of the pericardium

15.Which one of the following are blood vessels that carry blood away from the heart

A. Arteries

B. Capillaries

C. Veins

D. Coronary arteries

16. Blood vessels that return blood to the heart are called

A. Arteries

B. Veins

C. Capillaries

D. Pulmonary arteries

17. Venae cavae are the

A. Largest veins in the body

B. Smallest veins in the body

C. Longest veins in the body

D. Widest veins in the body

18. The longest veins in the body are

A. Venules

B. Capillaries

C. Venae cavae

D. Great saphaneous

19. _____ the outer layer of the blood vessel and sometimes called the tunica externa

A. Tunica intima

B. Tunica media

C. Tunica adventitia

D. None of the above

20. The middle layer of a blood vessel is called

   A. Tunica media

   B. Tunica adventitia

   C. Tunica intima

   D. All of the above

21. Tunica means

   A. A coat or layer of skin

   B. A coat or layer of tissue

   C. A coat or layer of muscle

   D. A coat or layer of fascia

22. Antecubital means

   A. Behind the knee

   B. In front of the knee

   C. In front of the elbow

   D. The other side of the ankle

23. _____ of the right ventricle forces the blood through the pulmonary semilunar

   valve into the pulmonary

   A. Laxation

   B. Contraction

C. Oxygen

D. Connection

24. The median cubital vein is

    A. Located on the medial aspect of the antecubital area

    B. Located in the lateral aspect of the antecubital area

    C. Located in the deep aspect of the antecubital area

    D. Located near the center of the antecubital area

25. The cephalic vein is

A. Located on the medial aspect of the antecubital area

B. Located in the lateral aspect of the antecubital area

C. Located in the deep aspect of the antecubital area

D. Located near the center of the antecubital area

26. The basilic vein is

    A. Located on the medial aspect of the antecubital area

    B. Located in the lateral aspect of the antecubital area

    C. Located in the deep aspect of the antecubital area

    D. Located near the center of the antecubital area

27. The first choice for venipuncture in the M-shape pattern because it is well anchored

    is the _____ vein

    A. Median

    B. Lateral

C. Deep

D. Center

28._____ are not use for routine blood collection

   A. Arteries

   B. Capillaries

   C. Veins

   D. Nerves

29. Thickening, hardening and loss of elasticity of artery walls is which of the following

   vascular system disorder

   A. Atherosclerosis

   B. Arteriosclerosis

   C. Varicose vein

   D. Aneurysm

30._____ is a mixture of fluid and cells

   A. Protein

   B. Blood

   C. Nutrient

   D. Plasma

31. The fluid portion of the blood is called

   A. Protein

   B. Nutrient

C. Calcium

D. Plasma

32. All of the following are sodium except

    A. Oxygen

    B. Potassium

    C. Calcium

    D. Magnesium

    E. Sodium

33. Erythrocytes are also known as

    A. Blue blood cells

    B. White blood cells

    C. Red blood cells

    D. Pink blood cells

34. The main function of white blood cells is to

    A. Paralyze or destroy pathogens

    B. Deodorize or destroy pathogens

    C. Neutralize or destroy pathogens

    D. None of the above

35. Which of the following is not a granulocytes

    A. Median vein

    B. Neutrophils

C. Eosinophils

D. Basophils

36. Monocytes are

    A. The largest WBCs

    B. The smallest WBCs

    C. The least numerous RBCs

    D. None of the above

37. Basophil have a life span of _____

    A. 6 hours to a few

    B. Varies from a few hours to a number of years

    C. Several days

    D. 6 hours to a few days

38. Monocytes have a life span of

    A. 6 hours

    B. Several months

    C. Several days

    D. Varies from a few hours to a number of years

39. The number of platelets in the blood of the average adult ranges from

    A. 140,000 to 400,000

    B. 150,000 to 400,000

    C. 151,000 to 400,000

D. 149,000 to 400,000

40. The most common blood type is

    A. O

    B. AB

    C. A

    D. B

41. The least common blood type is

    A. O

    B. AB

    C. A

    D. B

42. Platelets are actually part of a large cell called a

    A. Thrombocyte

    B. Granulocytes

    C. Megakaryocyte

    D. Monocyte

43. An individual whose RBCs lack the D antigen is said to be

    A. RX –

    B. RA-

    C. RB-

    D. RH-

44. Blood that have been remove from the body will coagulate or clot in _____ to _____ minutes

    A. 25, 60

    B. 30, 60

    C. 35, 60

    D. 40, 60

45. The remaining fluid portion of blood is called

    A. Serum

    B. Extra

    C. Milk

    D. Antibodies

46. An abnormal reduction in the number of RBCs in the circulating blood is called

    A. Thrombocytopenia

    B. Leukocytosis

    C. Leukemia

    D. Anemia

47. Leukopenia is

    A. An abnormal decrease in WBCs

    B. An abnormal increase in WBCs in the circulating blood

    C. An increased number of platelets

    D. A decreased number of platelets

48. Thrombocytopenia is

    A. An abnormal decrease in WBCs

    B. An abnormal increase in WBCs in the circulating blood

    C. An increase number of platelets

    D. A decreased number of platelets

49. Hemostasis means

    A. Loss of blood vessel

    B. The arrest or stoppage of plasma

    C. The arrest or stoppage of bleeding

    D. None of the above

50. Coagulation is the conversion of a liquid such as blood into a semisolid gel called a

    _____

    A. Serum

    B. Plasma

    C. Platelet

    D. Clot

51. Which of the following is not a step of the blood vessel repair

    A. Progression

    B. Formed elements

    C. Vasoconstriction

    D. Fibrinolysis

52. The main coagulation substrate is

    A. Fibrinogen

    B. Monocyte

    C. Leukocyte

    D. Element

53. Dia is a Greek word for

    A. Incomplete

    B. Through

    C. Around

    D. Surround

54. Extrinsic means

    A. Originating within

    B. Originating around

    C. Originating outside

    D. None of the above

55. Intrinsic means

    A. Originating within

    B. Originating around

    C. Originating outside

    D. Originating above

56. This phase begins with damage to blood vessel endothelial cells caused

A. Propagation phase

B. Amplification phase

C. Initiation phase

D. Basal phase

57. This phase involves another primary function of thrombin

A. Propagation phase

B. Amplification phase

C. Initiation phase

D. Basal phase

58. In this phase the large amounts of thrombin needed for fibrin formation are generated on the surface of activated platelets as more and more of them are drawn to the site of injury

A. Initiation phase

B. Basal phase

C. Propagation phase

D. Amplification phase

59. _____ is the process by which fibrin is dissolved

A. Thrombin

B. Hemostasis

C. Fibrinolysis

D. None of the above

60. The partition that separates the left and right side of the heart is called

    A. Interatrial septum

    B. Interventricular septum

    C. Atrioventricular septum

    D. Septum

61. Corona means

    A. Circle or crown

    B. Square or crown

    C. Croissant and crown

    D. None of the above

62. The electrocardiogram was formerly known as an

    A. EKG

    B. ETG

    C. EGG

    D. EEG

63. P waves are due to

    A. Ventricular repolarization

    B. Atrial depolarization

    C. Ventricular depolarization

    D. None of the above

64. The normal adult heart rate averages _____ beats per minute

A. 60

B. 70

C. 72

D. 100

65. Slow heart rate less than 60 beats per minute is called

A. Bradycardia

B. Tachycardia

C. Arrhythmia

D. Fibrillation

66. Fast heart rate over 100 beats per minute is called

A. Bradycardia

B. Tachycardia

C. Arrhythmia

D. Fibrillation

67. _____ are microscopic, one-cell-thick vessels that connect the arterioles and

venules

A. Veins

B. Nerves

C. Capillaries

D. Arteries

68. Fossa means

A. Hallow depression

B. Deep depression

C. Slight depression

D. Shallow depression

69. The average adult has from _____ to _____ WBCs per cubic millimeter

of blood

A. 5,000, 10,000

B. 51,000, 10,000

C. 6,000, 10,000

D. 7,000, 10,000

70. The ABO blood group system recognizes _____ blood types

A. Three

B. Two

C. Five

D. Four

71. The myocardium is the

A. Outer layer of the heart

B. Inner layer of the heart

C. Surrounded layer of the heart

D. Middle layer of the heart

1. _____ are substances used to prevent sepsis, which is the presence of

   microorganisms or their toxic products within the blood stream

   A. Antiseptics

   B. Disinfectants

   C. Biohazards

   D. None of the above

2. The antiseptic most commonly used for routine blood collection is _____ %

   isopropyl alcohol in individually wrapped prep pads

   A. 10

   B. 50

   C. 70

   D. 100

3. _____ are chemical substances or solutions regulated by the Environment

   Protection Agency (EPA) that are used to remove or kill microorganisms on surfaces

   and instruments

   A. Biohazards

   B. Antiseptics

   C. Alcohol

   D. Disinfectants

4. A _____ dilution is recommended for decontaminating nonporous surfaces after cleaning up blood or other body fluid spills in patient-care settings

    A. 1:10

    B. 1:100

    C. 1:1000

    D. 1:1

5. Which of the following organizations below recommend the use of alcohol-based hand sanitizers for routine decontamination of hands as a substitute for hand washing provided that the hands are not visibly soiled

    A. CDC

    B. OSHA

    C. FDA

    D. JCHO

6. _____ _____ should not be used on babies younger than 2 years of age because of the danger of aspiration and suffocation

    A. Cloth bandages

    B. Paper bandages

    C. Adhesive bandages

    D. Folded gauze

7. Which of the following containers below should be used when disposing used needles, lancets and other sharp objects

A. Dull containers

B. Sharps containers

C. Glass containers

D. Plastic containers

8. _____ are leak proof plastic bags that are commonly used to transport blood and other specimen from the collection site to the laboratory

   A. Biohazard bags

   B. Biohazard boxes

   C. Biohazard sheets

   D. All of the above

9. A phlebotomist should always carry a _____ with indelible no smear ink to label tubes and record other patient information

   A. Led

   B. Crayon

   C. Marker

   D. Pen

10. Transillumination means

    A. To inspect a muscle by passing light through its walls

    B. To inspect an organ by passing light through its walls

    C. To inspect the skin by passing light through its walls

    D. All of the above

11. A _____ is a device that is applied or tied around a patient's arm prior to venipuncture to restrict blood flow

    A. Tourniquet

    B. Rubber band

    C. Rope

    D. Ribbon

12. Which of the following is the most common type of tourniquet

    A. String

    B. Belt

    C. Strap

    D. Lace

13. A _____ can be used in place of a tourniquet

    A. Rope

    B. Blood pressure cuff

    C. Belt

    D. All of the above

14. The end of the needle that pierces the vein is called the _____ because it is "beveled" or cut on a slant

    A. Shovel

    B. Scoop

    C. Funnel

D. Bevel

15. The long cylindrical portion is called the _____

    A. Shovel

    B. Shaft

    C. Hub

    D. Lumen

16. The end that attaches to the blood collection device is called the _____

    A. Shaft

    B. Bevel

    C. Shovel

    D. Hub

17. The internal space of the needle is called the _____

    A. Scoop

    B. Shaft

    C. Lumen

    D. Hub

18. Which of the following needles is used on the veins of infant and children and on

    difficult or hand veins of adults

    A. Butterfly needle

    B. Hypodermic needle

    C. Multisample needle

D. Special needle

19. _____ needle is used primarily as a transfer needle rather than for blood collection

   A. Multisample

   B. Hypodermic

   C. Butterfly

   D. Special

20. Most multisample needles comes in _____ or _____ _____

   A. ½ to ¾ in. long

   B. 1 in.

   C. 1, 1.5 in. lengths

   D. 1.5 in.

21. Which of the following is responsible for clearing medical devices for marketing

   A. FDA

   B. JACHO

   C. FDN

   D. FTC

22. Evacuated tube system (ETS) needles that allow multiple tube of blood to be collected during a single venipuncture are called

   A. Safety needles

   B. Hypodermic needles

C. Butterfly needles

D. Multisample needles

23. A _____ _____ is a clear, plastic, disposable cylinder with a small threaded opening at one end where the needle is screwed into it and a large opening at the other end where the collection tube is placed

A. Board holder

B. Tube holder

C. Bag holder

D. Paper holder

24. OSHA acronym for a sharp is

A. SESEP

B. SISIP

C. SASAP

D. Sharp with engineered sharps injury protection (SESIP)

25. _____ _____ are used with both the ETS and the syringe method of obtaining blood specimens

A. Evacuated tubes

B. Evaluating tubes

C. Collecting tubes

D. Holding tubes

26. Evacuated tubes are filled with blood automatically because

A. There is suction

B. There is air

C. There is a vacuum

D. There is oxygen

27. Which of the following is a substance placed within a tube other than the tube

stopper

A. Additive

B. Coloring

C. Flavoring

D. None of the above

28. Light blue stopper color tubes are used in which department

A. Chemistry

B. Hematology

C. microbiology

D. Coagulation

29. Red stopper tubes have which of the following additive

A. Lithium

B. EDTA

C. Clot activator

D. Sodium heparin

30. Green stopper color tubes are used which department

A. Blood bank

B. Chemistry

C. Microbiology

D. Coagulation

31. Lavender/purple stopper tubes have which of the following additive

A. None

B. EDTA

C. Sodium citrate

D. Thrombin

32. Royal blue stopper color is used in what department

A. Chemistry

B. Blood bank

C. Coagulation

D. None of the above

33. Which of the following is the preferred method of blood collection

A. EVS

B. EVA

C. EVV

D. Evacuated tube system (ETS)

34. Syringes have _____ parts

A. One

B. Two

C. Four

D. Three

35._____ is a cylinder with graduated markings in either millimeters (ml) or cubic centimeters (cc)

A. Plunger

B. Drum

C. Barrel

D. Tube

36.A plunger is a

A. Rod shape device that fits tightly into the barrel

B. Cone shape device that fits tightly into the barrel

C. Square shape device that fits tightly into the barrel

D. Croissant shape device that fits tightly into the barrel

37.A _____ _____ _____ allows the safe transfer of blood into the tubes without using the syringe needle or removing the tube stopper

A. Plunger transfer device

B. Barrel transfer device

C. Volume transfer device

D. Syringe transfer device

38.A butterfly blood collection set is use for which of the following

A. Collecting blood from the elderly only

B. Coagulating specimen

C. Collecting blood from a decease patient

D. Collecting blood from small or difficult veins

39. Which of the is a tube manufacturer

A. Benton Dickinson

B. Becton Dickinson

C. Bacton Dickanson

D. Bector Dicanson

40. _____ are substances that prevent blood from clotting

A. Heparin

B. Citrates

C. Anticoagulants

D. None of the above

41. Which of the following are the most common coagulants

A. Citrates

B. Heparin

C. Oxalates

D. All of the above

42. Ethylenediaminetetraacetic acid is commonly available as a _____ or

_____

A. Powder, liquid

B. Gas, oil

C. Plastic, rubber

D. None of the above

43. If one of the following is found in a hematology specimen it cannot be used for

testing and must be recollected

A. Milli clots

B. Mini clots

C. Nano clots

D. Microclots

44. The most common citrate is _____

A. Sodium citrate

B. Calcium citrate

C. Potassium citrate

D. Oxygen citrate

45. Which of the following prevent clotting by inhibiting thrombin formation

A. Prozac

B. Kepra

C. Heparin

D. Phenobarbital

46. Heparin is an additive in all of the following except

A. Royal blue top tubes

B. Orange top tubes

C. Green/light green top tubes

D. Red banded top tube

47. Which of the following is not a heparin formulation

   A. Clorox 2

   B. Ammonium

   C. Lithium

   D. Sodium heparin

48. _____ is the most widely used oxalate

   A. Sodium oxalate

   B. oxygen oxalate

   C. Calcium oxalate

   D. Potassium oxalate

49. CPD is used in

   A. Collecting units of blood transfusion

   B. Collecting units of muscle transfusion

   C. Collecting units of gel transfusion

   D. None of the above

50. Which of the following prevents coagulation by binding calcium

   A. Acid citrate dextrose (ACD)

B. Citrate phosphate dextrose (CPD)

C. Sodium polyanethol sulfonate (SPS)

D. All of the above

51. An antiglycolytic agent is a substance that prevents which of the following

A. Osmosis

B. Photosynthesis

C. Glycolysis

D. Metabolism

52. The most common antiglycolytic agent is

A. Sodium fluoride

B. Sodium chloride

C. Potassium fluoride

D. All of the above

53. A _____ is a substance that enhances coagulation in tubes used to collect

serum specimens

A. Curl activator

B. Clot activator

C. Serum activator

D. Plasma activator

54. Silica particles cause the blood to clot within _____ to _____ minutes

A. 20, 25

B. 15, 20

C. 10, 30

D. 15, 30

55. Blood collected in thrombin tubes generally clots within _____ minutes

A. 5

B. 10

C. 6

D. 15

56. Which of the following is an inert synthetic substance initially contained in or near the bottom of certain blood collection tubes

A. Bio tropic gel

B. Thixotropic gel

C. Isotropic gel

D. None of the above

57. Kendal tubes with mottled red/gray rubber stoppers are called

A. Monterey jack tubes

B. Monoject korvac tubes

C. Monoject Corvac tubes

D. Serum separator tubes

58. Order to draw blood include all of the following except

A. Orange top coagulation tube

B. Sterile tube

C. Serum tube with or without clot activator, with or without gel

D. EDTA tube

59._____ is the transfer of additive from one tube to the next

A. Walkover/cross contamination

B. Slide over/ cross contamination

C. Hand over/ cross contamination

D. Carryover/ cross-contamination

60. The contaminating additive citrate test potentially affect which of the following test

A. Alkaline phosphatase

B. Calcium

C. Phosphorous

D. All of the above

61. The contaminating additive EDTA test potentially affect

A. Amylase

B. Red cell morphology

C. Creatine kinase

D. Urea nitrogen

62. The contaminating additive heparin test potentially affect which of the following

A. Protime

B. Sodium

C. Calcium

D. All of the above

63. The contaminating additive oxalates test potentially affect which of the following

A. Red cell morphology

B. Phosphorous

C. Sodium

D. Creatine kinase

64. _____ is a substance present in tissue fluid, activates the extrinsic coagulation

pathway and can interfere with coagulation tests

A. Paper thromboplastin

B. Cloth thromboplastin

C. Plastic thromboplastin

D. Tissue thromboplastin

65. What is the primary duty of a phlebotomist

A. To collect blood specimen

B. To collect urine specimen

C. To collect skin specimen

D. None of the above

66. Blood is collected by which of the following method

A. Arterial puncture

B. Capillary puncture

C. Venipuncture

D. All of the above

67. Which of the following organization regulates glove quality

    A. Occupational safety and health administration (OSHA)

    B. The centers for disease control (CDC)

    C. The U.S. food and drug administration (FDA)

    D. None of the above

68. Which of the following needles have the largest gauge

    A. 23 gauge

    B. 18 gauge

    C. 21gauge

    D. 20 gauge

69. Which of the following needles have the smallest gauge

    A. 18 gauge

    B. 20 gauge

    C. 21 gauge

    D. 23 gauge

70. Which of the following tubes have yellow tops and require eight inversions

    immediately after collection to prevent clotting

    A. Sodium polyanethol sulfonate (SPS)

    B. Citrate phosphate dextrose (CPD)

C. Oxalates

D. Acid citrate dextrose (ACD) tubes

SECTION THIRTEEN

1. _____ is the process of collecting or drawing blood from a vein and the most common way to collect blood specimens

A. Venipuncture

B. Vascular puncture

C. Oxalate

D. None of the above

2. Blood procedure legally begin with the _____

A. Book request

B. Paper request

C. Test request

D. All of the above

3. The acronym DAT means

A. Direct association test

B. Dialogue access testing

C. Direct Access Testing

D. None of the above

4. The form on which test orders are entered is called

   A. Recreation

   B. Regeneration

   C. Requisition

   D. None of the above

5. Required requisition information include all of the following except

   A. Patient date of birth or age

   B. Grandmother age

   C. Room number and bed

   D. Test status

6. A series of black strip stripes and white spaces of varying widths that correspond to letters and numbers is called

   A. Power code

   B. Stripe code

   C. Pin code

   D. Bar code

7. The process of recording in the order received is called

   A. Accession

   B. Recession

   C. Deception

   D. Contraception

8. The Latin word stat mean

    A. In a little while

    B. Immediately

    C. Before noon

    D. In two hours

9. Which of the following mean the same as stat

    A. Routine

    B. Timed

    C. Med Emerg

    D. Postop

10. Fasting means

    A. No food or drink except water for 8-12 hours

    B. Nothing by mouth

    C. Some food can be eaten

    D. All of the above

11. The Latin word nil per os means which of the following in English

    A. No food or drink

    B. Nothing before an operation

    C. Nothing food for three hours

    D. Nothing by mouth (NPO)

12. The acronym DNR means

A. Do not rest

B. Do no routine

C. Do not resuscitate

D. Do not respect

13. DNAR (do not attempt to resuscitate) means

    A. That there is an order stating that the patient should be resuscitate if he or she stops breathing

    B. That there is an order stating that the patient should not be revived if he or she stops breathing

    C. That there is an order that the patient should be revived at the request of a physician order

    D. None of the above

14. Which of the following indicate precautions against falling

    A. Fall trees

    B. Fall colors

    C. Fall leaves

    D. All of the above

15. A picture of a fallen leaf with a teardrop on it is sometimes used on obstetric wards to indicate that

    A. A patient has lost a baby

    B. A patient has lost a body part

C. The nurse has lost the patient

D. The doctor has lost the patient

16. Before entering a patient room it is a good idea to

    A. Just walk in

    B. To take visitors with you

    C. Knock lightly to make occupants aware that you are about to enter

    D. Both a and c

17. The behavior of a healthcare provider toward or as perceived by a patient is called

    A. Healthcare manner

    B. Bedside

    C. Manner

    D. Bedside manner

18. The patient must be involve in the identification process so when identifying a

    patient, ask the patient to

    A. Show his or her hospital chart

    B. Show proof of address and telephone number

    C. Show social security card

    D. State full name and date of birth

19. Patient ID band or bracelet is also called

    A. Leg band

    B. Neck band

C. Foot band

D. Arm band or wrist band

20. To avoid identification and mislabeling errors, some inpatient facilities require what

is referred to as

A. 2-Way ID

B. 1-Way ID

C. 3-Way ID

D. 4-Way ID

21. When identifying a patient never say

A. Are you Mrs. Smith?

B. May I check your ID band

C. Please state your name and date of birth

D. May I check your wrist band

22. Needle phobia means

A. Fear of hospital

B. Fear of needles

C. Fear of medication

D. None of the above

23. Which of the following is not a needle phobic symptoms

A. Profuse sweating

B. Nausea

C. Light-headedness

D. Red rash

24. A tourniquet is applied _____ above the intended venipuncture site to restrict venous blood flow and make the veins more prominent

A. 2 to 4 inches

B. 1 to 3 inches

C. 3 to 4 inches

D. 2 to 5 inches

25. Which of the following is not an example of the antecubital vein patterns

A. Z-pattern

B. H-pattern

C. M-pattern

D. Atypical

26. To palpate means

A. To examine by taste

B. To examine by smell

C. To examine by look

D. To examine by touch or feel

27. Which of the following means state of being freely open

A. Pattern

B. Patency

C. Pallor

D. Pulse

28. Which of the following is not include to prevent contamination of the site

A. Do not dry the alcohol with unsterile gauze

B. Do not fan the site with your hand or blow on it to hasten drying time

C. Blow on site to dry alcohol quickly

D. Do not touch the site after cleaning it

29. Which size winged infusion set (butterfly) is most commonly use

A. 23-gauge

B. 20-gauge

C. 18-gauge

D. 24-gauge

30. The needle sheath is the

A. Bevel

B. Shaft

C. Hub

D. Cap or covering

31. Which of the following is step 1 in the venipuncture process

A. Approach, identify and prepare patient

B. Review and accession test request

Verify diet restrictions and latex sensitivity

D. Reapply tourniquet, uncap and inspect needle

32. Thank the patient, remove gloves and sanitize hands is which step in the venipuncture process

    A. Step 4

    B. Step 9

    C. Step 19

    D. Step 2

33. Which of the following is step 8 in the venipuncture process

    A. Ask patient to remake a fist, anchor vein, and insert needle

    B. Establish blood flow, release tourniquet and ask patient to open fist

    C. Prepare equipment and put on gloves

    D. None of the above

34. Anchoring vein means

    A. Secure the vein firmly

    B. Holding the vein

    C. Putting pressure on vein

    D. Tapping the vein

35. Fill remove and mix tubes in order of draw or fill syringe is which step in the venipuncture process

    A. Step 13

    B. Step 7

C. Step 15

D. Step 8

36. Discard collection unit, syringe needle or transfer device is which step in the venipuncture process

    A. Step 16

    B. Step 19

    C. Step 2

    D. Step 14

37. Geriatric means

    A. Related to old skin

    B. Related to old age

    C. Related to old muscle

    D. Related to old hands

38. Clean and air dry the site is which step in the venipuncture process

    A. Step 5

    B. Step 9

    C. Step 11

    D. Step 7

39. Circles with a common center is known as

    A. Concentric circle

    Concern circle

C. Common circle

D. None of the above

40. Which of the following does an antiseptic do

A. It sterilize the site

B. Inhibit microbial growth

C. Inhibit fungus growth

D. Does none of the above

41. Which of the following test is used to diagnose or rule out syphilis, which can cause nerve damage and dementia

A. ESR

B. Glucose

C. VDRL/FTA

D. CBC

42. Which of the following test is use to determine hemoglobin levels, detect infection and identify blood disorders

A. CBC

B. Calcium/magnesium

C. ANAA, RA or RF

D. PT/PTT

43. Which of the following test identify abnormal levels associated with seizures and muscle problems

A. BUN/creatinine

B. ESR

C. Calcium/magnesium

D. CBC

44. Which of the following test detect inflammation

A. CBC

B. ESR

C. BUN

D. Glucose

45. Which of the following test diagnose lupus and rheumatoid arthritis, which can affect nervous system function

A. SPEP,IPEP

B. CBC

C. PT/PTT

D. ANA,RA or RF

46. Which two of the following diseases can affect speech

A. Diabetes

B. Lupus

C. Alzheimer's

D. Stroke and Parkinson's

~hould a blood collection tube be labeled

A. Just before the specimen is collected

B. Immediately after specimen is collected

C. As soon as the order comes in for the test

D. As soon as you get back to the lab

48. If a patient refused to have their blood drawn, which of the following should you do?

A. Notify the charge nurse or physician

B. Convince the patient to be cooperative

C. Use restrain and draw blood

D. Tell the patient that you will take him/her to dinner after the procedure

49. When you arrive to collect a stat hemoglobin specimen a physician or clergy is with the patient, what should you do?

A. Don't interrupt

B. Wait until they leave

C. Excuse yourself, explain why you are there and ask permission to proceed

D. Report to the charge nurse that you were unable to do the procedure

SECTION ONE

1. C
2. B
3. A

4. C

5. B

6. C

7. A

8. B

9. B

10. B

11. C

12. A

13. B

14. C

15. B

16. A

17. A

18. A

19. C

20. A

21. B

22. A

23. A

24. C

25. B

26. A

27. A

28. C

29. B

30. B

31. A

32. C

33. A

34. B

38.B

39.A

40.B

41.B

42.A

43.B

44.B

45.B

46.B

47.A

48.A

49.C

50.B

51.C

SECTION TWO

1. C	41. B
2. C	42. C
3. B	43. A
4. A	44. B
5. B	45. A
6. C	46. A
7. A	47. C
8. A	48. C
9. B	49. A
10.B	50. B
11.A	51. C
12.C	52. A
13.A	53. C
14.A	54. B
15.C	55. A
16.B	56. C

17.B

18.B

19.C

20.B

21.A

22.C

23.A

24.B

25.A

26.B

27.B

28.C

29.A

30.A

31.B

32.B

33.C

34.B

35.A

36.A

37.C

38.B

39.A

40.C

SECTION THREE

1. C	24. C	47. B	70. C
2. B	25. B	48. C	71. A
3. A	26. A	49. C	72. C
ʻ B	27. C	50. A	73. A
	28. B	51. A	74. B
	29. A	52. C	75. B
	30. B	53. A	76. A

8. B	31. C	54. B	77. C
9. A	32. A	55. B	78. A
10. C	33. C	56. A	79. B
11. B	34. B	57. C	80. C
12. C	35. A	58. B	81. B
13. B	36. B	59. C	82. B
14. C	37. C	60. A	83. C
15. A	38. A	61. B	84. A
16. B	39. C	62. C	85. A
17. A	40. A	63. B	86. B
18. C	41. C	64. A	87. C
19. C	42. B	65. A	88. C
20. B	43. A	66. A	89. A
21. B	44. B	67. C	90. C
22. A	45. A	68. B	91. B
23. C	46. A	69. A	92. A

93. A	118. B
94. A	119. B
95. C	120. C
96. A	121. A
97. A	122. B
98. B	123. C
99. C	124. B
100. B	125. A
101. A	126. C
102. C	127. A
103. A	128. C
104. A	129. B
105. C	130. B
106. C	131. A
107. B	132. C
108. A	133. B
109. B	134. A
110. C	135. C
111. B	136. B
112. B	137. C
113. A	138. B
114. C	139. A
115. B	140. C

116. A
117. C

SECTION FOUR

1. A	41. B	81. A
2. B	42. A	82. A
3. C	43. A	83. C
4. B	44. C	84. B
5. C	45. A	85. C
6. B	46. B	86. A
7. A	47. A	87. A
8. C	48. A	88. B
9. A	49. B	89. C
10. A	50. B	90. A
11. B	51. C	91. B
12. C	52. A	92. B
13. B	53. B	93. A
14. B	54. A	94. C
15. C	55. C	95. B
16. A	56. C	96. A
17. A	57. A	97. B
18. C	58. C	98. A
19. A	59. B	99. C
20. C	60. A	100. C
21. B	61. B	101. B
22. B	62. A	102. A
23. C	63. C	103. B
24. B	64. A	104. C
25. B	65. B	105. C
26. A	66. A	106. B
27. C	67. B	107. C
28. C	68. A	108. B
29. A	69. C	109. A
30. C	70. B	110. C

31.B   71. B
32.A   72. A
33.C   73. C
34.A   74. A
35.B   75. B
36.B   76. C
37.C   77. B
38.C   78. B
39.B   79. A
40.B   80. A

SECTION FIVE

1. C   41. C   81. B
2. A   42. B   82. B
3. B   43. A   83. A
4. B   44. C   84. C
5. C   45. B   85. A
6. A   46. A   86. C
7. C   47. A   87. A
8. A   48. B   88. B
9. C   49. A   89. C
10.A   50. A   90. B
11.C   51. B   91. C
12.C   52. C   92. B
13.B   53. B   93. B
14.A   54. C   94. A
15.B   55. A   95. C
16.B   56. A   96. A
17.B   57. A   97. C
18.C   58. A   98. B
19.A   59. B   99. A
20.C   60. C   100. A
21.A   61. A

22.B	62. C
23.C	63. B
24.A	64. A
25.B	65. A
26.B	66. C
27.A	67. A
28.C	68. A
29.A	69. B
30.A	70. B
31.C	71. B
32.B	72. A
33.A	73. C
34.B	74. C
35.B	75. B
36.C	76. C
37.B	77. B
38.A	78. A
39.C	79. A
40.B	80. C

SECTION SIX

1. D
2. B
3. A
4. C
5. D
6. A
7. D
8. D
9. B
10. A
11. C
12. C
13. A

14. D
15. A
16. B
17. D
18. A
19. C
20. D
21. A
22. C
23. B
24. D
25. D
26. B
27. B
28. C
29. C
30. D, I
31. A, E
32. G
33. H
34. B, F
35. A
36. C
37. B
38. D
39. D
40. B
41. A
42. B
43. D
44. A
45. A
46. A
47. B
48. C
49. A
50. C

51. A

52. B

53. A

54. D

55. B

56. D

57. B

58. C

59. B

60. A

61. C

62. B

63. C

64. D

65. A

66. C

67. A

68. D

69. D

70. B

71. C

72. C

73. A

74. A

75. A

SECTION SEVEN

1. A

2. C

3. B

4. C

5. D

6. B

7. C

8. A
9. A
10. A
11. B
12. A
13. C
14. B
15. D
16. D
17. A
18. C
19. B
20. A
21. B
22. D
23. A
24. D
25. B
26. D
27. D
28. C
29. A
30. D
31. C
32. A
33. D
34. B
35. C
36. A
37. D
38. C

SECTION EIGHT

1. D

2. C
3. B
4. B
5. C
6. D
7. A
8. C
9. B
10. C
11. A
12. D
13. A
14. B
15. C
16. B
17. D
18. D
19. A
20. B
21. D
22. A
23. C
24. C
25. C
26. A
27. D
28. B
29. D
30. C
31. B
32. B
33. A
34. B
35. B
36. A
37. A

38. D
39. D
40. A
41. A
42. B
43. C
44. D
45. B
46. B
47. A
48. D
49. B
50. C
51. C
52. C
53. D
54. A
55. B
56. A
57. C
58. B
59. A
60. D
61. C
62. C
63. D
64. A
65. B
66. B
67. A
68. B
69. B
70. C
71. A
72. D
73. C
74. C

75.D
76.A
77.A
78.A
79.D
80.C
81.B
82.B
83.D
84.B
85.D
86.C
87.A
88.A

SECTION NINE

1. C
2. C
3. D
4. A
5. A
6. B
7. A
8. D
9. C
10.B
11.A
12.D
13.C
14.B
15.A
16.B
17.A
18.D

19.C

20.B

21.A

22.D

23.C

24.B

25.A

26.C

27.B

28.A

29.D

30.C

31.B

32.A

33.D

34.C

35.B

36.A

37.B

38.B

39.B

40.C

41.D

42.A

43.A

44.C

45.D

46.A

47.B

48.A

49.D

50.C

51.B

52.A

53.D

54.C

55.B

56.A

57.D

58.C

59.B

60.A

61.D

62.C

63.B

64.A

65.D

66.C

67.B

68.A

69.D

70.C

71.B

72.A

73.D

74.C

75.B

76.A

77.A

78.A

79.D

80.B

81.C

82.D

83.D

84.A

85.B

86.D

87.D

88.C

89.D

90.A

91.C

92.C

93.C

94.D

95.B

96.A

97.C

98.D

99.D

100.   C

101.   C

102.   A

103.   B

104.   C

105.   B

SECTION TEN

1. A

2. D

3. A

4. C

5. A

6. B

7. A

8. C

9. D

10.C

11.A

12.B

13.C

14.D

15.C

16.C

17.B

18.B

19.D

20.B

21.A

22.D

23.A

24.D

25.B

26.C

27.D

28.C

29.A

30.A

31.C

32.B

33.D

34.A

35.A

36.C

37.B

38.D

39.D

40.A

41.C

42.B

43.A

44.D

45.D

46.C

47.B

48.B

49.A

50.B

51.A

52.D

53.C

54.D

55.A
56.B
57.A
58.D
59.C
60.B
61.C
62.A
63.A
64.B
65.B
66.D
67.A
68.D
69.D
70.C
71.B
72.A
73.B
74.D
75.C
76.C
77.D
78.B
79.A

SECTION ELEVEN

1. A
2. D
3. B
4. C
5. D
6. A
7. C
8. C

9. B
10. D
11. B
12. C
13. C
14. D
15. A
16. B
17. A
18. D
19. C
20. A
21. B
22. C
23. B
24. D
25. B
26. A
27. A
28. A
29. B
30. B
31. D
32. A
33. C
34. C
35. A
36. A
37. C
38. B
39. B
40. A
41. B
42. C
43. D
44. B

45.A

46.D

47.A

48.D

49.C

50.D

51.B

52.A

53.B

54.C

55.A

56.C

57.B

58.C

59.C

60.D

61.A

62.A

63.B

64.C

65.A

66.B

67.C

68.D

69.A

70.D

71.D

SECTION TWELVE

1. A

2. C

3. D

4. B

5. A

6. C
7. B
8. A
9. D
10. B
11. A
12. C
13. B
14. D
15. B
16. D
17. C
18. A
19. B
20. C
21. A
22. D
23. B
24. D
25. A
26. C
27. A
28. D
29. C
30. B
31. B
32. A
33. D
34. B
35. C
36. A
37. D
38. D
39. B
40. C
41. D

42. A
43. D
44. A
45. C
46. B
47. A
48. D
49. A
50. C
51. C
52. A
53. B
54. D
55. A
56. B
57. C
58. A
59. D
60. D
61. C
62. D
63. A
64. D
65. A
66. D
67. C
68. B
69. D
70. D

SECTION THIRTEEN

1. A
2. C
3. C
4. C

5. B
6. D
7. A
8. B
9. C
10. A
11. D
12. C
13. B
14. C
15. A
16. C
17. D
18. D
19. D
20. C
21. A
22. B
23. D
24. C
25. A
26. D
27. B
28. C
29. A
30. D
31. B
32. C
33. C
34. A
35. A
36. D
37. B
38. D
39. A
40. B

41. C
42. A
43. C
44. B
45. D
46. D

OTHER TITLES FROM THE SAME AUTHOR:

1. Jokes for Nurses

2. Work At Home Jobs For Nurses

3. How Nurses Can Make Money Online

4. Director of Staff Development: The Nurse Educator

5. Crisis Prevention & Intervention in Healthcare: Management of Assaultive Behavior

6. CNA Exam Prep: Nurse Assistant Practice Test Questions. Vol. One and Two

7. Patient Care Technician Exam Review Questions: PCT Test Prep

8. IV Therapy & Blood Withdrawal Review Questions

9. Medical Assistant Test Preparation

10. EKG Test Prep

11. Phlebotomy Test Prep

12. The Home Health Aide Textbook

13. How to make a million in nursing

Order these books now at www.bestamericanhealthed.com/resources.html
Or call 951 637 8332 for bulk purchases

Order these books at www.bestamericanhealthed.com/resources.html

Or call 951 637 8332 for bulk purchase

8522627R00137

Made in the USA
San Bernardino, CA
11 February 2014